MW01168340

BEGINNER'S GUIDE

TO

ADOBE

PHOTOSHOP

2025

Master Essential Settings, Tools, Layers, Image Adjustments, and
Creative Techniques with Troubleshooting Tips Included

Copyright © 2024 **Miles Greywood**

All Rights Reserved

Any reliance you place on such information is therefore strictly at your own risk. In no event will the author or publisher be liable for any loss or damage including, but not limited to, indirect or consequential loss or damage, or any loss or damage whatsoever arising from loss of data or profits arising out of or in connection with the use of this book.

Disclaimer and Terms of Use

The information contained in this book is for general informational purposes only. While every effort has been made to ensure that the content is accurate and up-to-date, the author and publisher make no representation or warranties of any kind, express or implied, about the completeness, accuracy, reliability, suitability, or availability concerning the book or the information, products, services, or related graphics contained in the book for any purpose.

Printed in the United States of America

TABLE OF CONTENTS

INTRODUCTION

Adobe Photoshop 2025 represents a whole new frontier in digital creativity, offering innovative tools and much more efficient workflows that target making creative work easier and more enjoyable for both beginners and professionals alike. One of the longest-standing standard-bearers among graphic editors has, with this new release, developed its reputation even further by featuring advanced capabilities to simplify many tasks, improve overall performance, and enhance flexibility across platforms. This update retains its two-fold utility by allowing professionals to perform edits with high-class precision and beginners to easily perform edits through intuitive controls. Photoshop 2025 combines classic editing features with innovative AI capabilities in a manner that this creative space strikes a balance between imagination and technical development, thus enabling users to turn their imagination into reality even more smoothly and effectively. The most striking feature of Adobe Photoshop 2025 is the increasing number of AI-driven tools available within it. These enhancements range from improved object selection and smart masking through background removal, to making editing easier and allowing users to apply complex changes with minimal effort. Adobe has also honed its neural filters to deliver effects that adjust portraits, lighting conditions, and even the ambiance of landscapes-enabling changes like switching the time of day. These features also let creatives step back and visualize the more artistic portions of a project, while still allowing users at any skill level to edit details.

Adobe Photoshop 2025 also boasts updated core editing tools and new options for blending modes and layer management, all separate from AI. An extended library of blending modes, coupled with increased control over depth, texture, and visual effects, comes with several presets designed for easy integration across multiple layers. The ability to couple these blending modes with enhanced masking features enables users to compose complex images in a snap. Such updates will surely help photographers working in difficult lighting conditions and designers making intricate, multilayered designs to add a new dimension of precision to the creative process.

Photoshop 2025 is about to be nothing short of second-to-none regarding performance and cross-platform compatibility, featuring advanced cloud integrations that will make seamless transitions between desktops, tablets, or mobile devices easy. This will entail a seamless workflow where artists can start a project on one device and pick up right where they left off on another without loss of data or quality compromise. Match that with advanced export settings and color management options, and Photoshop 2025 goes fully kitted for creatives to produce professional work, whether in a studio or on the go. Continuing to drive home flexibility and user experience, Adobe continues to push the boundaries of digital art and design, furnishing users with the tools they need to innovate in an ever-evolving creative landscape.

CHAPTER ONE

GETTING STARTED WITH PHOTOSHOP 2025

NEW FEATURES

Photoshop 2025

Adobe Photoshop 2025 introduces a host of exciting features with the aim of user experience improvement and smoothing the creative workflow. The following are highlights of that release:

1. **Distraction Remove Tool:** This intelligent tool automatically identifies and removes unwanted objects, for example, people, wires, or background objects. It can work both in generative AI and traditional modes, respectively, depending on which will work best given the context of the image, delivering smooth and seamless edits.

2. **Improved Generative Fill and Expand**: Using the newest Image Model from Adobe Firefly, these features have greatly improved photorealism and responsiveness with intricate prompts, making expansion or modification of image content much easier.

3. **Generate Similar Variations**: With Variations, users can generate numerous variations of an image by accessing the several ways in which tools such as the Generative Fill or Expand can create variations, thereby providing even more options for experimentation.

4. **Generate Background**: AI-powered, the feature replaces backgrounds with minimum toil and with depths, shadows, and lighting that best match the subject in focus, thus strikingly balanced compositions with little effort.

5. **OpenColorIO and 32-bit HDR Support**: Support for OpenColorIO means users will have much better control over color within Photoshop across other applications. More tools will now be supported for 32-bit HDR images; hence, high-fidelity editing capability without compromising image quality.

6. **Improved Font Browser with Variable Fonts:** An enhanced font browser with premium fonts, including Variable Fonts, paired with an enhanced search option to quickly select fonts either by name or other attributes.

7. **Generative Workspace (Beta):** A beta workspace designed to facilitate ideation by enabling users to create creative assets from text prompts, explore multiple ideas at once, and maintain a vetted history of created content.

8. **Adobe Substance 3D Viewer (Beta):** This new stand-alone desktop app easily brings 3D assets into the design as editable Smart Objects, and stitches together 2D and 3D design workflows in a seamless way.
9. **Contextual Taskbar Enhancements:** Contextual Task Bar will show more intuitive step suggestions depending on user workflow, and common functionalities with fewer clicks.
10. **Improved Gradient Tool**: The Gradient tool now offers on-canvas controls, live previews, and non-destructive editing, giving users a wider capability to create gradients more flexibly and accurately.

CREATING A NEW DOCUMENT

Adobe Photoshop 2025 makes creating a new document even easier with the addition of more templates and customizable presets. Instead of starting from scratch, users can avail themselves of a wide range of Adobe Stock templates that are pre-designed assets and illustrations ready to be edited. These open as normal **.psd files**, include several artboards, and are very flexible to work within any project. A user can use Photoshop's preset options or create custom sizes and save those as reusable presets, affording both inspiration and efficiency when setting up documents.

Templates

Not only does working with templates save time, but seeing design elements within your workspace often sparks creativity and inspires developers to morph them into something that will work for any given project. Whether you begin with a preset or download quality graphics from Adobe Stock, Photoshop's templates prove to be a versatile starting point, ensuring that every project begins with a strong, visually cohesive base.

Blank Document Preset

Photoshop has something to make life easier, too; it's called Blank Document Presets, which means to already have the document set up with a myriad of different formats concerning several devices and projects. Such presets make things easier in designing since they are all set to have the optimal dimensions and attributes for specific applications, such as a template for an iPad Pro layout. Once these pre-set settings are used, the settings will already include document size, color mode, units, orientation, resolution, and many more. However, there is still some degree of flexibility, as any setting within a preset can be changed before the document is created, so each project should be aligned with its particular needs.

Types of Presets Available in Photoshop

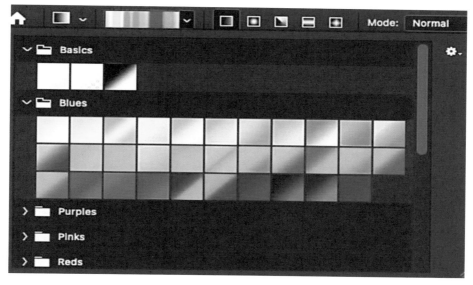

Photoshop organizes preset documents into various categories that fit specific design uses. **These include:**

- **Photo**: This pertains to photography projects, sizes, and resolutions relevant to high-quality images.
- **Print**: This is set up for print projects with settings mostly for CMYK mode and high DPI for clarity.

- **Art & Illustration**: Enables digital painting and illustration, selecting various canvas sizes and color modes.
- **Web**: This is for web graphics and layouts, mostly in RGB color mode to keep compatibility with screen displays.
- **Mobile**: Includes popular dimensions and device specifications for the creation of mobile applications or interfaces.
- **Film & Video**: Offers presets for standard video resolution, aspect ratios, and color profiles for video.

Opening the New Document Dialog in Photoshop

To access these presets, open the New Document dialog in Photoshop from one of the following:

1. Open **Photoshop 2025**.
2. **To open a new document, do one of the following:**
   - Use the keyboard shortcut **Cmd+N (Mac)** or **Ctrl+N (Windows).**
   - Go to **File > New**.
   - Click **New** in the **Start** workspace.
   - Right-click any open document tab and click **New Document** from the menu.

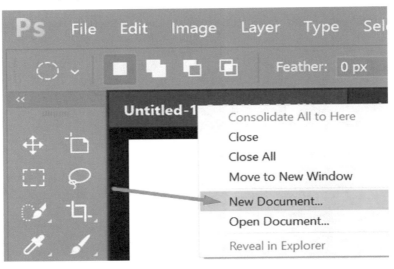

New Document Dialog Overview

The New Document dialog opens several options to start a new project in Photoshop:

- Preset templates should be selected to view Adobe Stock templates under categories like Photo, Print, Web, etc., which are already loaded with graphics, fonts, and layouts.

- The **Recents** tab allows one to reach recent files or templates used in previous projects.

- Save and load your own presets so you can reuse the same settings over and over.

- Once a preset category, such as Photo, Print, or Web has been selected, select a preset that best fits your purpose. Then later, when opening a document, adjust those settings to better fit your design needs.

Creating a New Document Using Presets

1. To open a new document using a preset, click a category such as **Photo, Print, or Web** in the New Document dialog box.

2. Scroll through and click a preset that is closest to your needs for a project.

3. Select size, color mode, and orientation as well as other options that are specific to the preset within the Preset Details pane.

4. Click **Create** to produce the document with your modified preset settings.

Modifying and Editing Presets

When opening a preset, you might like to edit the preset settings within the Preset Details pane first:

1. Select your file name for the new document.

2. **Modify any of the other options that appear in the dialog depending on the kind of preset including:**
   - **Width and Height**: Set the document size and its measurement unit.
   - **Orientation**: Select Landscape or Portrait orientation.
   - **Artboards**: Check this box if your design requires the opening of multiple artboards in one document.
   - **Color Mode**: Choose a color mode, which includes RGB, CMYK, and Grayscale.
   - **Resolution**: Set the quality of the image by changing the DPI.
   - **Background Contents**: Choose the default background color.

3. If you want further options, click the Advanced Options to choose settings such as:

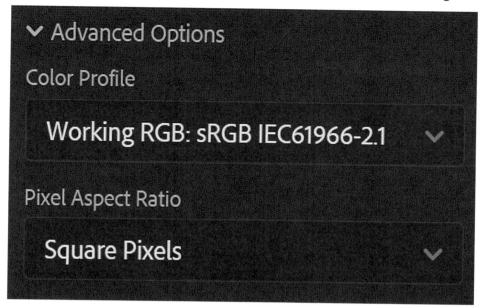

- **Color Profile:** Select the color profile to ensure proper color management.
- **Pixel Aspect Ratio:** Specify the aspect ratio for pixels, which is required when designing videos and broadcasts.

Saving Your Custom Presets

If you have already adjusted a preset and would like to save it to use again later on:

1. In the Preset Details pane, click the **save** ⬇ **icon.**
2. Name your new preset and click **Save Preset**. This custom preset will now be available to you from the Saved tab in the New Document dialog.

USING ADOBE STOCK TEMPLATES IN PHOTOSHOP

Photoshop has thousands of templates courtesy of Adobe Stock, which will help make designing for a beginner and pro much easier to navigate through the design process. To access a template in Photoshop, **follow these steps:**

1. Open the **New Document dialog** and select a category tab.

2. Scroll through and select a template.

3. Click **See Preview** to view a template. If you like it click Download.

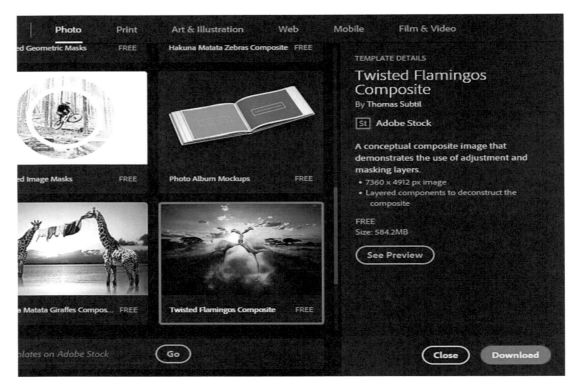

Photoshop will ask you if you need to license the template.

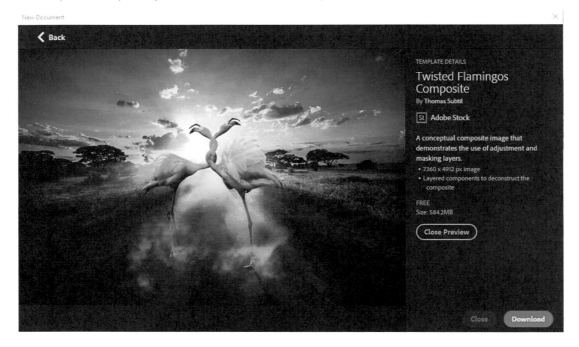

4. Once downloaded, click **Open** to edit the template in a Photoshop document (.psd).

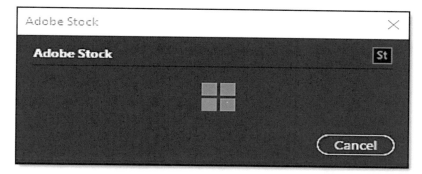

Searching Adobe Stock for Additional Templates

Beyond the default option, you might want to search Adobe Stock for even more templates:

- Type a search term in the **Find More Templates** on **Adobe Stock box**, or click **Go** to open the Adobe Stock website and view even more templates that are available to download.

Opening the Legacy New Document Experience

To access the legacy File New experience offered in older versions of Photoshop (before 2015.5), do the following in Photoshop:

1. Select **Edit > Preferences > General**.

2. Check **Use Legacy File New Interface** and click **OK**.

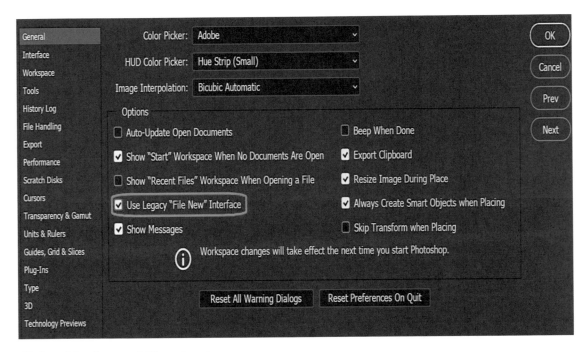

Editing Keyboard Shortcuts

Photoshop gives you a lot of flexibility in creating your keyboard shortcuts:

1. To open the Keyboard Shortcuts dialog box, go to **Edit > Keyboard Shortcuts**.

2. From the pop-up menu at the top, choose a set of shortcuts (Application Menus, Panel Menus, Tools, or Task Spaces).

3. Edit or add new keyboard shortcuts. If a keyboard shortcut is already assigned to another command, you will get an alert that allows you to go on and edit the conflicting key or undo your action.

PLACING FILES AS SMART OBJECTS

Photoshop allows the addition of external files as Smart Objects - upon transforming, quality is maintained:

- Open any document in Photoshop.
- Go to **File > Place Embedded** and **File > Place Linked**.
- In the opened window select the file you will place and click Place.
- **Establish properties:** position, scale, etc according to your needs.
- For PDF and Illustrator files, by clicking on **Place** you will be able to change some settings in the Place PDF dialog before placing it.

Pasting Adobe Illustrator Art

You can copy and paste directly out of Illustrator into Photoshop:

Smart Object

When you place artwork as a Smart Object in Photoshop, the design becomes embedded as a vector-based layer. You can scale, rotate, and move the layer around, and it won't impact image quality. It retains vector properties, meaning increased and decreased sizes do not lose clarity or sharpness. But as a Smart Object, the data in this art file remains separate within the document of Photoshop, its independent layer, which means you can always go back to that original, untouched version if you need to at any time.

Pixels

Pasting artwork as Pixels places the content directly onto a new layer within the document, where it becomes pixel-based. By doing this, you will be able to transform the art-resize and reposition it before fixing its position. If rasterized, it stays as a static image that is not editable in terms of vector scaling. This option is best used when the goal is to embed the art as a fixed object that aligns with other pixel-based content.

Path

When pasting as a Path, the artwork is taken as an editable outline so that you can easily make alterations to it with the help of the Pen tool, Path Selection tool, or the Direct Selection tool. It also embeds in the selected layer of the Layers panel. In the case of complex designs where paths are very useful, minute readjustments may be required, these give precision to reshape or change the position of any single segment of the outline.

Shape Layer

When you paste as a Shape Layer, the artwork comes in as a new layer with a path and fills it with the foreground color. With this, you can make solid fills, gradients, or even pattern overlays keeping your shapes editable by editing via anchor points or by reediting the fill style at any time.

After selecting either Smart Object or Pixels from within the Paste dialog box, transforms can be applied, resized, rotated, or repositioned before confirming placement with **Enter** or **Return**.

PLACEMENT WITH GUIDES AND GRIDS

Placement with guides and a grid is gold when it comes to the precise placement of elements. Guides are non-printing lines that can float above the workspace to maintain consistency in element alignment. You can move them where you want and even lock them to prevent them from accidentally moving. Smart Guides are dynamic guides that automatically align your shapes and selections when you create or move them to provide a more accurate layout.

The grid is a symmetric reference structure that displays as lines or dots to keep your imagery balanced and symmetric.

Guides and Grids share some similarities in that they:

- Snapping Selections and tools will **"snap"** to a guide or grid line when dragged near it, providing a quick way to align objects precisely.

- **To customize the grid spacing and/or guide snapping behavior for any project:** The grid and guide styles are universal, but spacing and visibility can be determined on a per-document basis.

Hiding and Showing Guides and Grids

1. **To toggle guides, grids, or Smart Guides on and off:**
   - **Guides**: To show or hide guides go through **View > Show > Guides**.
   - **Grid:** To show or hide the grid go through **View > Show > Grid**.
   - **Smart Guides**: To toggle Smart Guides, go through **View > Show > Smart Guides**.
   - **Extras**: To turn visibility on and off for other elements such as layer and selection edges choose **View > Extras**.

Viewing and Creating Guides

To show a guideline, rulers need to be on (**View > Rulers**). To be able to view the precise alignment of objects, zoom into **100%** view or use the Info panel.

To Create a Guideline:

- **New Guide**: Go to **View > Guides > New Guide** and choose orientation and set position/color.
- **Drag from Ruler:** Simply click and drag from the horizontal or vertical ruler to set a guide.

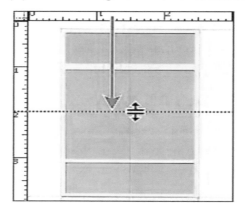

You can draw guides horizontally and vertically with snapping behavior that also can be adjusted, and lock guides (**View > Guides > Lock Guides**) to prevent them from moving.

Guides

Moving guides including editing and removal:

- **To move a guide**: With the **Move tool** ⊕ active click and drag, or use the hotkey **Ctrl/Command**.

- **To rotate a guide**: **Alt/Option-drag** will toggle between horizontal and vertical orientation.

Edit Guides

- To modify the color, position, or other options for guides, right-click and select the option to open **Edit Selected Guides**.

Delete Guides

- To delete guides, drag a guide from the image area or select **View > Guides > Clear Guides** and select all guides or selected guides to delete them.

Adjusting Guide and Grid Preferences

- To modify the grid and guide colors, styles, and spacing select **Edit** (Windows) or **Photoshop** (Mac) **Menu > Preferences > Guides, Grid, & Slices**.

You can:

- Choose colors or create custom colors.

- Indicate the style of guides or grid.

- Indicate grid intervals and subdivisions for the presentation of accurate layout divisions.

- These settings can make the workspace more personalized hence increasing productivity and better visualization.

Enhanced Guide Capabilities

Color-coding of guides is now possible in Photoshop. This enhances identification, particularly in complex layouts.

- A new dialog box called the **Edit Selected Guides dialog box**, makes for quick adjustments of guide color orientation and other properties.
- Multiselect guides using **Alt+Shift (Windows)** or **Option+Shift (Mac)** for batch editing.

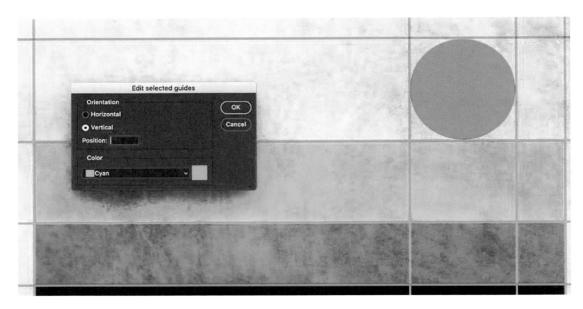

EXPORTING PHOTOSHOP IMAGES TO OTHER APPLICATIONS

The application is very well integrated with other Adobe applications, such as InDesign: There is the possibility of direct import from Photoshop (PSD) files. Layers, masks, and effects will be preserved. InDesign will correctly show transparency, hence extra formatting may not be required. In page layout programs that do not support PSD files:

- **Create Clipping Paths**: A clipping path to define where transparent backgrounds are located so they will appear correctly.

- **Save in Supported Formats**; To assure maximum compatibility, save as and choose TIFF if printing on non-PostScript printers or EPS on a PostScript printer.

Use Photoshop Artwork in Illustrator

Photoshop files are smoothly integrated into Adobe Illustrator, making it simple to use Photoshop pictures without changing their format. Photoshop (PSD) files may be opened or placed immediately into Illustrator, allowing users to import intricate images for additional creative work.

Illustrator gives you the option of linking an image to preserve the integrity of the original file or embedding it as part of the document. While embedding integrates the image as a static element, linking enables you to make modifications to the image in Photoshop and have those changes mirrored in Illustrator. Simply use Illustrator's **"Edit Original"** command to edit a linked image, which opens the file in Photoshop. Illustrator automatically updates the file when you save it after making changes.

How to Import Photoshop Documents

1. Close the Photoshop file after saving it in the PSD format.
2. Select an import option from the list below in Illustrator.
3. Choose **File > Open,** find the file, and click **Open** to open it straight.
4. Select **File > Place**, open the Illustrator file, deselect Link to embed, and then click Place to add the image.
5. Use **File > Place**, choose connection, and then click **Place** to place an image while keeping a connection to the original file. The image is linked if there is a red "**X**" across it, which means Photoshop is required for editing.
6. Illustrator displays a Photoshop Import dialog box when embedding an unlinked image, allowing you to choose from:
    *   Converting **Photoshop Layers to Objects** preserves transparency and some effects while maintaining individual layers as editable objects in Illustrator.
    *   To simplify the design, flatten Photoshop layers to a single image. This preserves the visual integrity of the design but eliminates the option to adjust individual layers.

Creating Transparency Using Image Clipping Paths

When you need to make portions of an image translucent for layout applications, image clipping paths come in handy. By eliminating extraneous backgrounds and exposing only the foreground, clipping paths highlight the main topic.

When a Photoshop image has to blend in perfectly with Illustrator or another program, this technique is really helpful. Nevertheless, because clipping paths are vector-based, they result in hard-edged transparency, which means that subtle changes like shadows are lost.

 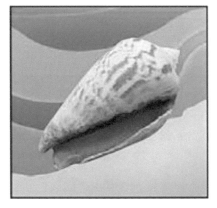

Create a Path for Clipping:

1. Set a work path around the portion of the image that you wish to keep.
2. In the Paths window of Photoshop, save the path.

3. Choose the stored path, choose **Clipping Path** from the panel menu, and, if necessary, change the Flatness option. Smoother curves are produced with a lower flatness setting, which is perfect for high-resolution printing.
4. Save the file in the proper format, such as TIFF for non-PostScript outputs or EPS, DCS, or PDF for PostScript printers, to guarantee compatibility with different printing techniques.

Printing Image Clipping Paths

Complex clipping paths may result in printing issues, especially when using high-resolution printers.

Make clipping paths simpler by:

- Lowering the path's anchor points by hand.
- When making paths, increase the tolerance level; for smoother curves, start with 4-6 pixels.

Exporting Paths to Illustrator from Photoshop

To easily merge artwork from Photoshop and Illustrator, Photoshop paths may be exported to Illustrator. For example, you can use Photoshop's Pen tool to create a path, and then convert it to Illustrator components for exact alignment.

To export paths to Illustrator, follow these steps:

1. In Photoshop, create and save a path.

2. To save, pick the Work Path after selecting **File > Export > Paths to Illustrator**.

3. To further adjust the path or align items as necessary, open the produced file in Illustrator.

Embedding or Linking Photoshop Documents

Photoshop files may be linked or embedded into Windows programs such as Microsoft Word, Adobe FrameMaker, or PageMaker by using OLE (Windows Only) OLE (Object Linking and Embedding) capabilities.

Whereas embedding keeps the file static inside the document, linking preserves a dynamic connection to the original file. Double-clicking the Photoshop file once it has been linked or embedded allows you to modify it in Photoshop, and any changes are mirrored in the host program.

Modifying Embedded or Linked OLE Objects

1. To open the embedded or linked image in Photoshop, double-click on it.

2. Close the file or choose **File > Update** after making changes to embedded pictures.

3. Update the file in the container application after saving and closing the file containing linked pictures.

Use the Undo or Redo Commands

To Reverse or Redo an Operation, Follow These Steps:

- **Undo**: Reverses the undo chain by one step. Use the keyboard shortcut **Control + Z** (Windows) or **Command + Z** (Mac) or select **Edit > Undo**.

- **Redo**: Advances one step. Use the keyboard shortcut **Shift + Control + Z** (Windows) or **Shift + Command + Z** (Mac) or select **Edit > Redo**.

The name of the step that will be undone is also shown next to the Undo and Redo options in the Edit menu.

Cancel an Operation

- Hold down **Esc** until the current action is over. You may also use **Command+period** with Mac OS.

Get Alerted When an Operation Is Finished

An operation is being carried out when a progress bar appears. You have the option to stop the process or have the application alert you when it is complete.

1. Take one of these actions: Select either **Photoshop > Preferences > General** (Mac OS) or **Edit > Preferences > General** (Windows).
2. Choose **Beep** When Completed.
3. Press **OK**.

HOW TO USE THE HISTORY PANEL

Any recent version of the image made during the current working session may be accessed via the History panel. Every time you modify an image, the panel is updated with the image's new state.

- For instance, the panel lists each of the stages that occur when you pick, paint, and rotate a portion of an image. The image returns to its original appearance after you choose one of the states. After that, you may work from there.
- In Photoshop, the History panel can also be used to create a document from a state or snapshot and to remove image states.
- Either click the **History panel tab** or select **Window > History** to bring up the History panel.

When using the History panel, bear the following in mind:

- Since they are not modifications to a specific image, program-wide changes—such as those made to panels, color settings, actions, and preferences—do not appear in the History panel.
- The History section automatically displays the last 20 states. By selecting an option under **Preferences > Performance**, you can change the quantity of remembered states. To give Photoshop additional memory, older states are automatically removed. Take a picture of the condition you want to maintain during your work session.
- All states and snapshots from the most recent working session are removed from the panel when you close and reopen the document.
- By default, the top of the panel shows a snapshot of the document in its original condition.
- The list now includes states at the bottom. This means the oldest state is at the top and the newest state is at the bottom of the list.
- The name of the tool or command used to alter the image is mentioned for each condition.
- When you choose a state, the states beneath it are automatically darkened. In this manner, you may quickly observe which modifications will be removed if you keep working in the chosen state.
- By default, all subsequent states are removed when a state is chosen and the image is changed.
- You can use the **Undo command** to reverse the most recent alteration and restore the states that were removed if you choose a state and then modify the image, removing the states that followed.
- When a state is deleted, it automatically removes all subsequent states as well. Deleting a state only removes that state if you select the **Allow Non-Linear** History option.

How to Start Using the History Panel

Launch Photoshop and Select your Project.

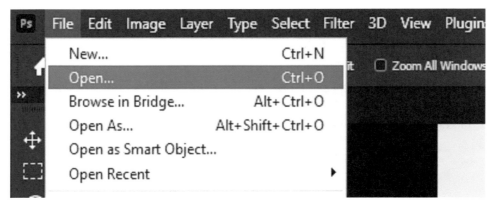

Get the History Panel open.

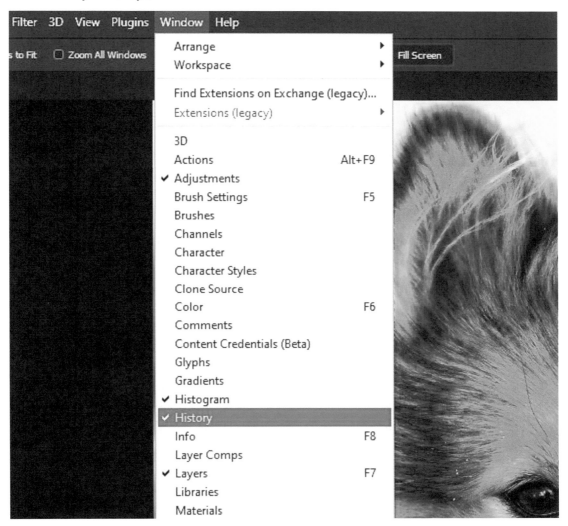

Setting History States

- You can choose how many history states to record in Photoshop.
- To change this setting, select **"Edit" > "Preferences" > "Performance" (Windows)** or **"Photoshop" > "Preferences" > "Performance" (Mac).**

Remember, more history states mean greater memory.

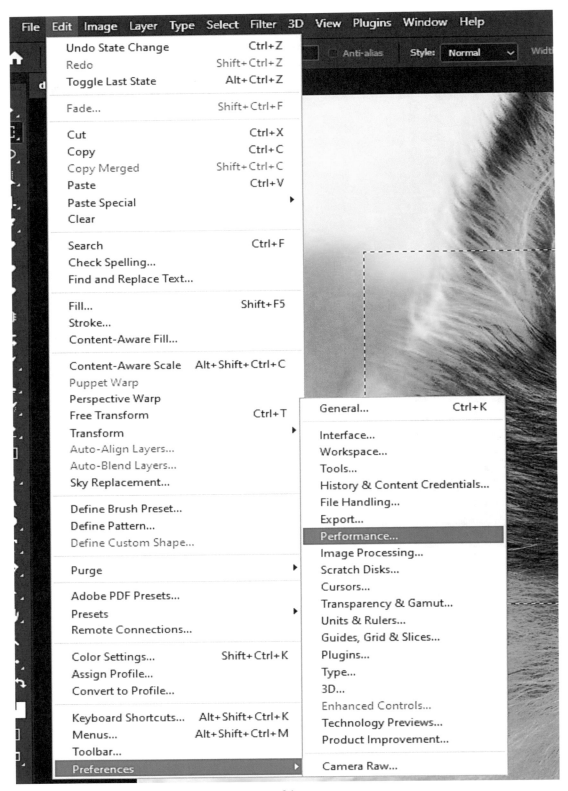

Revert to a Previous Image State

Take one of the Following Actions:
- Select the state's name.
- To get to the next or previous state, select **Step Forward** or **Step Backward** from the History panel menu or the **Edit menu**.

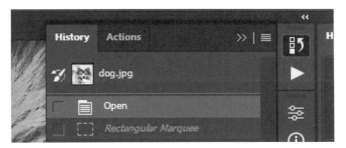

Delete one or more Image States

Take one of these actions:
- To remove that update and any subsequent ones, click the state's name and select Delete from the History panel menu.

- To remove that modification and any subsequent ones, drag the state to the **Delete symbol** 🗑 .

- To remove the list of states from the History panel without altering the image, **select Clear History** from the panel menu. Photoshop's memory use is unaffected by this setting.

- To remove the list of states without altering the image, select **Clear History** from the panel menu while holding down **Alt** (Windows) or **Option** (Mac OS). Purging states is helpful if you receive a notification that Photoshop is running low on memory since it clears out memory by deleting the states from the Undo buffer. The **Clear History command** cannot be reversed.

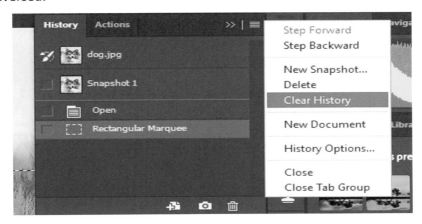

- To remove all open documents' states from the list, select **Edit > Purge > Histories**. This action cannot be reversed.

Create or Replace a Document with an Image State

Take one of these actions:
- In the History panel, drag a state or snapshot onto the "**Create A New Document from Current State** 🖼 " button. Only the Duplicate State entry appears in the freshly formed document's history list.

- Click the "**Create A New Document from Current State** 🖼 " button after selecting a state or snapshot. Only the Duplicate State entry appears in the freshly formed document's history list.

- From the History panel menu, choose **New Document** after selecting a state or snapshot. Only the Duplicate State entry appears in the freshly formed document's history list.

- Drag a state onto a document that already exists.

Note

It is recommended that you create a new file for each state you save to store one or more snapshots or image states for use in a subsequent editing session.

Make sure to open the other saved files when you reopen the main file. To view the snapshots again from the History panel of the original image, drag the first snapshot of each file to the original image.

Set History Options

The History panel can be customized by setting various parameters and a maximum number of things to display.

1. From the History panel menu, select **History Options**.
2. Choose an option:

Create the First Snapshot Automatically

- When the document is opened, a snapshot of the image's initial state is automatically created.

Create a New Snapshot Automatically

- Every time you save, a snapshot is generated.

Allow Non-Linear History

Makes modifications to a chosen state without erasing subsequent states. Typically, all states that follow the selected state are erased when you choose a state and alter the image. A list of the editing steps in the order they were made may then be seen in the History panel.

Nonlinear state recording allows you to pick a state, alter the image, and then remove that state alone. At the end of the list is an appendix with the change.

- **Make Layer Visibility Changes Undoable**
  By default, this option is selected. As a historical phase, turning on or off-layer visibility is noted.
  To avoid layer visibility changes in history steps, **deselect this option**.

Set Edit History Log options

For your personal records, client records, or legal requirements, you might need to maintain meticulous records of all the modifications made to a Photoshop file. You may maintain a written record of all image modifications with the use of the Edit History Log. The Edit History Log metadata may be seen using the **File Info dialog box** or Adobe Bridge.

The information can be stored in the metadata of changed files, or it can be exported to an external log file. File size increases when several editing activities are stored as file metadata; these files may take longer to open and save than usual.

Note: Use Adobe Acrobat to digitally sign the log file after preserving the edit log in the file's metadata if you need to demonstrate that it hasn't been altered.

Each session's history log data is automatically stored as metadata that is integrated into the image file. You can choose the amount of information in the history log as well as where the data is stored.

1. Select either **Photoshop > Preferences > General** (Mac OS) or **Edit > Preferences > General (Windows).**

2. Toggle the **History Log** option from on to off or the other way around.

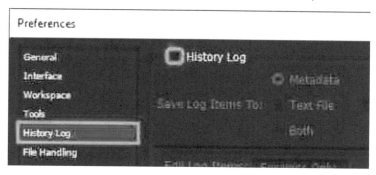

3. Select one of the following options for the Save Log Items To option:

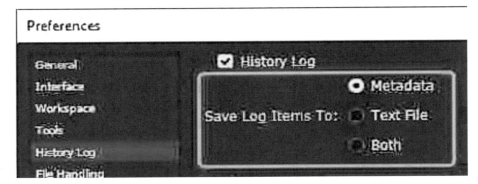

Metadata

- Keeps the history log in each file as embedded information.

Text File

- The history log is exported to a text file. You are asked to select a place for the text file's storage and give it a name.

Both

- Stores a text file and stores metadata in the file.

Note: Click the **Choose button**, enter the place where you want the text file to be saved, give it a name if needed, and then click Store if you want to store it somewhere else.

Select one of the following choices from the Edit Log Items menu:

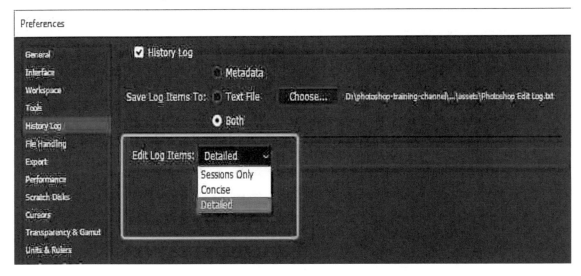

- **Sessions Only**
  Maintains a log of every time you launch or exit Photoshop and every time you open and close files (including the filename of each image).
- **Concise**
  Concise contains both the session information and the text that shows in the History panel.
- **Detailed**
  Consists of both the Concise information and the language that shows in the Actions panel. Select **Detailed** if you want a comprehensive history of all file modifications.

Make a Snapshot of an Image

You can create a temporary duplicate (or snapshot) of any image state with the **Snapshot command**. The History panel's top snapshot list now includes the newly inserted snapshot. By choosing a snapshot, you may work with that particular image.

Similar to the states seen in the History panel, snapshots provide the following benefits:

- Snapshots can be saved for a whole work session; you can readily compare impacts; and you can name a snapshot to make it easier to recognize.

- You may, for instance, capture a picture both before and after using a filter. Next, pick the first picture and experiment with the same filter under other conditions. To choose the settings you like, flip through the photos.

- Snapshots make it simple to recover your work. Before applying an action or experimenting with a sophisticated approach, take a picture. You can choose the snapshot to reverse every stage if you're unhappy with the outcome.

It should be noted that when an image is closed, its snapshots are also deleted. Additionally, choosing a snapshot and altering the image removes every state that is now displayed in the **History panel** unless you use the Allow Non-Linear History option.

Create a Snapshot

1. Choose a state and take one of the actions listed below:
- Click the **Create New Snapshot button** in the History panel to have a snapshot created automatically, or if Automatically Create New Snapshot Select New Snapshot from the History panel menu after Saving has been chosen in the history options.
- You may either **Alt-click (Windows)** or **Option-click (Mac OS)** the Create New Snapshot button to choose parameters when taking a snapshot, or you can select New Snapshot from the History panel menu.

2. Type the snapshot's name into the Name text field.

3. From the menu, choose the contents of the snapshot:

- **Full Document**
  Captures a picture of the image's layers in that condition.
- **Merged Layers**
  Creates a snapshot in which every layer in the image is combined at that point.
- **Current Layer**
  Captures a snapshot of just the layer that is presently chosen in that state.

How To Work with Snapshots

Take one of the actions listed below:

- To choose a snapshot, either click on its name or move the slider to the left of it up or down to pick a different snapshot.

- Double-clicking a snapshot and entering a new name will rename it.

- To remove a photo, either drag the snapshot to the **Delete icon**, click the **Delete icon** 🗑 , or pick **Delete** from the panel menu.

Paint with a State or Snapshot of an Image

You can paint a duplicate of an image state or snapshot into the active image window using the **History Brush Tool** ✍. This tool creates a sample, or copy, of the image and uses it to paint.

A snapshot of a modification you made using a painting tool or filter, for instance, might be created (with the Full Document option selected at the time of creation). You might use the History Brush tool to apply the modification to certain sections of the image after reversing the original alteration. The History Brush tool paints from a layer in the selected state to the same layer in another state unless you choose a merged snapshot.

Only at the same spot can the History Brush tool copy across states or snapshots. To create distinctive effects in Photoshop, you may also paint using the Art History Brush tool.

1. First, choose the **History Brush tool** ✍ .

2. In the options bar, select one of the following actions:

- Select a brush and specify brush parameters.

- Indicate the blending mode and opacity.

3. Select the state or snapshot that will serve as the source for the History Brush tool by clicking on its left column in the History panel.

4. Use the History Brush tool to paint by dragging.

CHAPTER TWO

LAYERS

USING LAYERS IN PHOTOSHOP

To perform actions like compositing numerous photos, adding text to an image, or creating vector graphic forms, use layers. You may sharpen objects or apply layer styles for extra effects like a glow or drop shadow. A layer's opacity can also be altered to partly transparentize its contents.

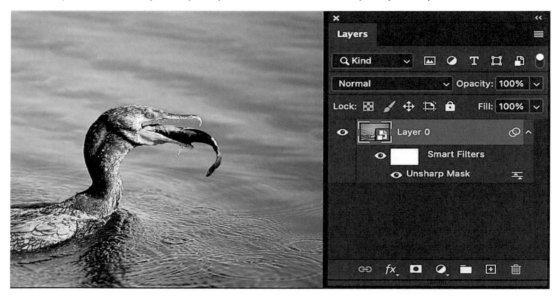

Objects in natural images can be made to stand out with sharp details. Use the Unsharp Mask filter to emphasize the details in non-destructive layer modifications.

Use Layer Groups to Organize and Manage Layers

When working on a new image, you often begin with a single layer. Your creativity mostly determines how many layers, layer effects, and layer sets you may add.

Use groups to intelligently arrange layers and minimize panel clutter. Manage and arrange layers in the Layers panel. Groups may be nested and used to apply masks and attributes to many layers at once.

Use Layers to Carry Out Non-Destructive Editing

- **Adjustment layers:** Modify your image's colors and tones without causing any permanent changes to the pixels. You can continue to work on the adjustment layers. To put it briefly, they provide more flexibility and control over image alterations than direct adjustments.

- **Smart objects**: Layers containing image data from vector or raster images are known as smart objects. They allow you to make non-destructive changes to the layer while maintaining the original qualities of the image's underlying material.

HOW TO WORK WITH THE LAYERS PANEL

- To examine, create, and modify layers, layer groups, and layer effects in your image, use the Layers panel.

- Pressing **F7** or going to **Window > Layers** will activate this panel.

- To apply layer effects, interact with a layer group, convert to a smart object, and create a new or duplicate layer, use this menu.

- This option also allows you to change the thumbnails' size. Choose the desired thumbnail, then adjust the size using the right-click menu.

Modify the Contents of the Thumbnail

To view the contents of the full document, choose **Entire Document** from the Layers panel menu's panel options. To limit the thumbnail to the object's pixels on the layer, choose **Layer Bounds**.

Note: To reduce canvas space and enhance speed, you may also disable thumbnails.

Filter Layers

To find important layers in complicated documents, use the filter options at the top of the Layers window. To display a subset of layers, use the provided options **Kind, Name, Effect, Mode, or Artboard.**

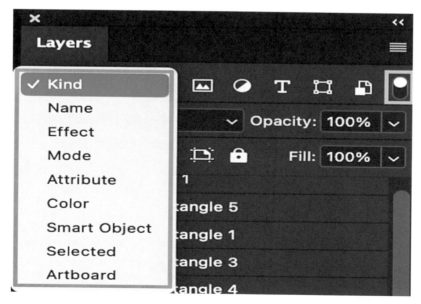

Toggle between layer filters using the toggle switch in the Layers panel.

1. From the pop-up menu, select a filter type.

2. Choose or input the filter parameters.

3. Toggle the layer filtering on or off by clicking the toggle switch.

Video Layers

With video layers, you can include a video into an image.

Once a video clip has been imported as a video layer into an image, you can accomplish the following:

- Mask or change the layer

- Apply layer effects

- Individual frames can be painted on or rasterized and then converted to a standard layer.

To view individual frames or play the movie inside the image, use the **Timeline window**.

Create a New Layer when Brushing

A vector layer is the sort of layer on which text and objects are automatically produced. A vector layer always maintains its clean edges no matter how far you zoom in.

Photoshop turns a vector layer into pixels when you rasterize it. Zooming in on a freshly rasterized layer will reveal that the edges are now composed of small squares called pixels, even if you might not notice the change at first.

Only rasterized layers may be used with some tools, such as brush tools, erasers, paint bucket fill, and filters. A vector layer must first be transformed into pixels to use one of these tools.

Be advised that a vector layer loses its vector capabilities when it is converted to pixels. This means that:

- Text is no longer editable, which means that you cannot alter the font or the words.

- Shapes and text cannot be resized to any size without sacrificing quality.

Create an empty layer above the vector layer and use any of the painting or drawing tools on the new layer instead of rasterizing to paint or draw directly on the vector layer.

Paint on the new layer with the Brush Tool after selecting the New Layer icon in the Layers menu.

Another option is to go to **Preferences > General > Create a new layer when brushing**. If enabled, all brushstrokes will be applied to a new pixel layer that is automatically formed in the layer stack when brushing on a layer that cannot be painted on (such as a smart object, type, or adjustment layer) or when no layer is active.

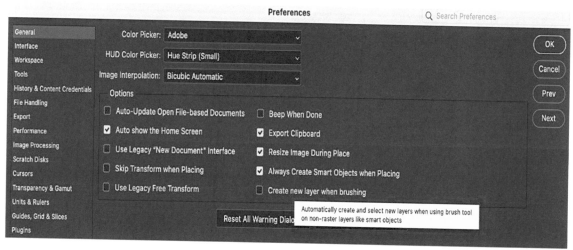

Go to **General > Preferences > Create a new layer when brushing** to automatically disable the preference.

Convert Photoshop Layers and Background

The background is the first (bottom-most) layer when making a new image with a colorful or white backdrop. There can only be one background layer in an image.

You can transform the background layer into a regular layer and then edit its properties, but you can't change its blending mode, opacity, or stacking order.

There is no backdrop layer when a new image with transparent content is created. This layer's blending mode and opacity can be adjusted anywhere in the Layers panel.

To turn the background layer into a normal layer, use the following actions:

1. Either select **Layer > New > Layer from Background** or double-click Background in the Layers window.
2. Configure the layer settings.
3. Click **OK**.

To turn an Ordinary Layer into the Backdrop Layer, take the following actions:

1. In the Layers panel, select the standard layer.

2. Select **Layer > New > Layer Background**.

The layer falls to the bottom of the layer stack once any transparent pixels are changed to the background color.

Note: The **background From Layer command** must be used to create a backdrop; a standard layer cannot be named Background.

Make Duplicate Layers in Photoshop

Layers can be copied into a new image, into another image, or inside an existing image.

Duplicate a group or layer in Photoshop inside an image:

In the Layers panel, pick a layer or group.

Take one of these actions:

- Drag the group or layer to the button labeled "**Create a New Layer.**"
- Or, from the Layers menu or Layers panel menu, select **Duplicate Layer** or **Duplicate Group**. After giving the layer or group a name, click OK.

Duplicate a Photoshop layer or group in another image

1. Launch the destination and source pictures.

2. Choose one or more layers, or a group of layers, from the source image's Layers window.

Take one of these Actions:

- From the Layers panel, drag the layer or group to the desired image.

- Alternatively, you can drag from the source image to the target image by using the **Move tool**. In the destination image's Layers panel, the duplicate layer or group is seen above the current layer. If the pixel dimensions of the source and destination pictures are the same, you may use shift-drag to move the image content to the same spot in the source image; if not, you can move it to the center of the document window.

- Or, from the Layers menu or Layers panel menu, select **Duplicate Layer** or **Duplicate Group**. From the Document pop-up menu, pick the destination document, then click OK.

Create a New Document out of a Group or Layer in Photoshop

1. From the Layers panel, choose a **layer** or **group**.

2. From the Layers menu or Layers panel menu, select **Duplicate Layer** or **Duplicate Group**.

3. From the Document pop-up menu, choose **New**, then click **OK.**

Sample from all Visible Photoshop Layers

- With the Mixer Brush, Magic Wand, Smudge, Blur, Sharpen, Paint Bucket, Clone Stamp, and Healing Brush tools, you can only sample or smudge color from pixels on the current layer.
- Choose **Sample All Layers** from the options bar to blur or sample pixels from every visible layer using these tools.

Changing Transparency Preferences

The steps:

1. To access **Transparency & Gamut** in Photoshop on macOS, navigate to **Edit > Preferences > Transparency & Gamut** on Windows.

2. To hide the transparency checkerboard, select None for Grid Size or select the transparency checkerboard's size and color.

3. Click **OK**.

INTRODUCTION TO LAYERS: HOW TO CREATE, EDIT, AND ORGANIZE LAYERS

Creating Layers

Layers are easily created in Photoshop, but each different layer type adds a different dimension to your work and is used for different reasons, including:

Types of Layers:

- **Pixel Layers:** These are the normal kinds of layers that you will be painting, drawing, or adding images directly into. Pixel layers often make up the base of your design.

- **Adjustment Layers:** These layers apply color or tonal adjustments to an image and don't permanently affect the actual pixel data. They work quite well when performing color correction or enhancing an image.

- **Text Layers:** When you insert text, by default, Photoshop will create a text layer. You can then edit the text independent of the rest of the pixels that may be present on the other layers.

- **Shape Layers:** When you insert a vector shape, a shape layer gets created, and unlike pixel-based layers, vector shapes will not lose their quality when you zoom in and out.

- **Smart Object Layers:** These are used to retain the original data of an image. This allows you to apply non-destructive transformations and filters easily.

How to Create New Layers:

- To open a new layer, from the Layers panel, click the '**+**' icon at the bottom. Alternatively, one may go to **Layer > New > Layer**, or by **Shift+Ctrl+N** if on Windows or **Shift+Cmd+N** if on Mac.
- A pop-up window opens that creates a name for your layer, allows you to set its opacity, and even allows you to pick a color with which you may visually organize it.

As each layer is automatically added on top of the currently selected layer in the Layers panel, remember that the order of the layers controls how the content of your project appears, so pay attention to the layer's order.

Editing Layers

Editing of layers is where the flexibility of Photoshop comes into play. You can also manipulate a layer since each is separate without disturbing other parts of your composition.

- **Move Layers:** Use the Move tool by selecting V. It is particularly useful when you want to shift any of the elements across a layout.

  Holding down the **Shift key** while you are moving constrains the layer to go horizontally or vertically.

- **Layer Transformation:** You can scale, rotate, or distort a layer within **Edit > Free Transform**, using **Ctrl+T or Cmd+T.**

  The handles can be dragged to resize, and holding Shift constrains the proportions. A right-click on the layer shows the other options: skew, distort, and perspective.

- **Blending Modes**: Blending modes are how a layer interacts with the layers below it. A good example could be Multiply, which will darken the layer, while Screen will lighten it.

  Blending mode options can be found at the top of the Layers panel. Among many, try Overlay, Soft Light, and Difference for unusual effects.

- **Opacity and Fill**: Lowering the opacity of a layer makes it more transparent, allowing layers underneath to show through; fill affects only the transparency of the pixel content, not the layer effects.

- **Layer Masks:** Another feature in editing allows a user to mask in or out parts of any layer without the creation of destruction.

  Adding a mask is done by selecting a layer and then clicking on the mask icon in the Layers panel. Paint with black on the mask to hide areas, paint with white to reveal them.

- **Layer Styles:** The added effects of shadow, stroke, and glow bring great things to your work.

  You can simply double-click on the layer to apply a style, or you can go to **Layer > Layer Style**. Each effect you edit brings full control over color, opacity, distance, and a lot more.

Organizing Layers

As your project gets larger, organizing layers for better efficiency and clarity becomes very important.

Rename Layers: If it is necessary to rename any layer, simply double-click the name of the layer; for instance, "**Main Text**" or "**Background Image**," so that in complicated projects, the designer can recall the contents of the layers.

Grouping Layers: With this option, you group related layers into groups. It's really useful for cleaning up the Layers panel. You can hold **Ctrl or Cmd** while clicking to select more than one layer.

Then you will use **Ctrl+G for Windows** and **Cmd+G for Mac** to create a group. Groups can be assigned their opacity, blending mode, and layer styles, allowing uniform adjustments among all the layers in the group.

Layer Folders: Like groups, folders are also holders of layers and groups, introducing another degree of organization for complex projects. The folder feature is very helpful for designers who have to deal with a large number of elements in one project.

Color Coding: Color codes are another great way to differentiate between layers at one glance. Right-click on any layer and select Layer Properties to choose a color. You could color code all text layers blue and all images green.

Locking Layers: You can lock layers to prevent edits from being made to them inadvertently.

Options include the following options to lock:

- **Transparent Pixels**: It doesn't allow the editing of the transparent area.
- **Image Pixels:** This prevents the editing of the image pixels of the layer.
- **Position**: This will lock the position of the layer but allow editing of other attributes.
- **Full Lock**: Everything gets locked, and you cannot edit the layer.

Layer Comps: This allows you to create multiple versions of a layout within a single file. In Photoshop, Layer Comps captures the layer's visibility, position, and appearance which is useful when exploring variations of your design.

CHAPTER THREE

BASIC TOOLS FOR BEGINNERS

OVERVIEW OF BASIC SELECTION TOOLS: MOVE, MARQUEE, AND LASSO

For over a decade, Adobe Photoshop has been a powerhouse in the field of digital image editing. The most basic ingenuity of Photoshop involves selection tools, which are meant to help users filter parts of an image for editing purposes. Basic selection tools are the Move Tool, Marquee Tool, and Lasso Tool-all of which contribute a distinctive capability to create, manipulate, and perfect visuals.

These tools have further been refined in Adobe Photoshop 2025 to make selections easier, quick, and even more accurate. Let's dig deeper into the explanation of each of these essential tools, and their functions, and give some quick tips on how to derive the most from them.

The Move Tool

The Move Tool is one of the most used tools inside Photoshop. It is a cross-shaped cursor with an arrow at each end. As the name would suggest, the primary function of the Move Tool is to move selected parts of an image, layers, and selections. You can activate the Move Tool via your keyboard by pressing the "**V**" key or from the top of the Tools panel.

Key Features and Usage

- **Move Layers and Selections:** Under the Move Tool, you can move any layer or selection anywhere around within your canvas. This comes in handy if you are going to set up any element in any composition - maybe align a text layer, or place a graphic element inline.
- **Alignment Options**: The Move Tool has options for alignment, especially for a set of layers. You can center-align, align, distribute, and arrange elements accurately by selecting two or more layers and clicking the alignment buttons in the Options bar.

- **Auto-Select and Show Transform Controls:** Some advanced settings of the Photoshop 2025 Move Tool are **"Auto-Select"**, which allows you to select any layer just by clicking on it without actually entering the Layers panel.

  "Show Transform Controls" allows you to resize or rotate a layer or selected area by moving handles that pop up around your selection, offering finer control over the transformation adjustment you are trying to do.

The Marquee Tool

The Marquee Tool is one of the easiest selection tools in Photoshop that provides options to select from rectangular to elliptical and even single-row or column selections. This will enable you to select a geometric form in no time, and quite conveniently when selecting huge areas or backgrounds. The Marquee Tool could be accessed via **"M"** or by clicking it in the Tools panel.

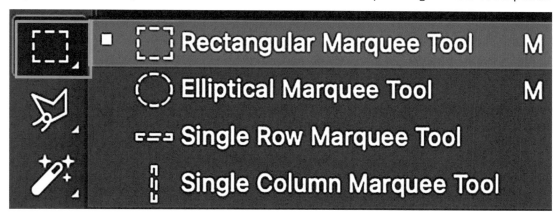

Key Features and Usage

- **Rectangular and Elliptical Marquee Selections**: The Rectangular Marquee Tool will select in a rectangle or square; the Elliptical Marquee Tool will select in a circle or ellipse. Holding down the Shift key when operating these tools constrains the selection to a perfect square or perfect circle.

- **Single-row and Single-column Marquee Tools**: These are the variants of the tool that enable you to select a single row or column of pixels, hence, assisting in drawing thin lines or patterns across the canvas.

- **Feathering and Anti-Alias:** The Marquee Tool in Photoshop 2025 can allow feathering that in turn softens the edges of a selection. It helps in the smoother blending of the selection with its surroundings. Anti-aliasing creates softer edges in selections. This in turn is quite helpful in selections of an elliptical nature due to the potential of distracting jagged edges.

The Lasso Tool

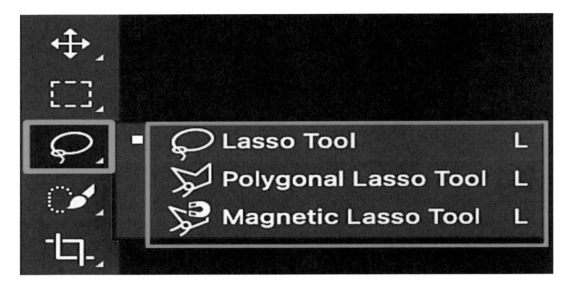

The Lasso Tool is one of the most versatile selection tools in Photoshop; it allows a user to make freehand selections. It is particularly useful in selecting objects of irregular shape and for making complex selections when the geometric shapes just won't work. Adobe Photoshop 2025 offers three variants of the Lasso Tool: normal, the Polygonal Lasso Tool, and the Magnetic Lasso Tool.

Key Features and Usage

- **Basic Lasso Tool:** The basic Lasso Tool allows for a freehand selection, which means that you can draw with your cursor around the portion you would want to select. This tool is handy in working out shapes that do not have strict boundaries and require more organic outlines.
- **The Polygonal Lasso Tool**: This is an ideal variant of selections containing a straight edge; you can click around the area creating a series of straight-line segments. Once a double click is made, this selection will automatically close into a polygon.
- **Magnetic Lasso Tool**: An intelligent tool following the edges of objects by "**snapping**" to them as one traces around the area of selection. Ideal in selecting high-contrast areas, it works by recognizing and following edges due to the difference in contrast (for example, the subject from the background).

WORKING WITH BASIC SHAPES, TEXT, AND DRAWING TOOLS

Working with Basic Shapes

Shapes are one of the basic elements of almost any design project - as a base for creating logos, icons, banners, and more. Recently, Photoshop 2025 has overhauled its shape creation and manipulation interface, making the process seamless and effortless with several attached tools and features.

- **Shape Tool Options**: The options available in Photoshop 2025 Shape Tools are Rectangle, Ellipse, Polygon, Line, and Custom Shape. To use this, one needs to select the Shape Tool from the toolbar; U is the shortcut for selection. On selecting, a drop-down menu opens to choose the shape.

- **Create a Shape:** Click on the canvas and drag anywhere to create a shape. If you hold the Shift key, it constrains the proportions, which will give you a perfect square or a circle. If you need a size, you can simply specify it in the options bar.

- **Shape Properties Panel**: Once a shape has been created, the Shape Properties panel opens up, from which one can alter the stroke, fill, and dimensions of the created shape. Photoshop 2025 further extends color options for stroke and fill-in the form of gradients and patterns. Corner radii can be specified for rectangles, thus allowing for rounded corners.

- **Shape Transformations**: The powerful options for transforming shapes are contained in Photoshop. Make the Transform option available via **Edit > Transform** by scaling, rotating, and skewing a shape. You also can do it manually using the Free Transform Tool Ctrl + T or Cmd + T on Mac.

- **Shape Layers**: Each shape is on a separate vector layer. This always allows you to go back and edit any shape properties without loss of quality because it's non-destructive. If you want to manage shapes together, group them using Ctrl + G or Cmd + G on Mac.

Using Text Tools

Text is so important in projects from website design to social media graphics. The enhanced Type Tool in Photoshop 2025 will allow for a more intuitive interface for adding text and styling it.

- **Type Tool Basics**: The Type Tool (T), is located in the toolbar. Click on the canvas to create a point text that will allow you to type a line of text. Alternatively, drag to create a text box for paragraph text, which is ideal for larger bodies of text.

- **Text Properties Panel: The** Properties panel will enable you to edit font, size, color, alignment, and also tracking once you have typed. Photoshop 2025 offers support for more fonts, extending to an even more enhanced font library provided by Adobe, integrated with variable fonts. You can change the weight, width, and slant, giving you more freedom with typography.

- **Paragraph Styles and Alignment**: This gives you control over text alignment by justifying options via the Paragraph Panel. You are also capable, in Photoshop, of creating and saving your text styles so you can apply a consistent look across many text layers with ease.

- **Text Warping Options**: Under **Type > Warp Text**, Photoshop provides **'Warp Text'**, which offers some preset distortions like Arc, Bulge, and FishEye for creating dynamic titles and headers for styled text.

- **Text Transformations and Effects**: The blending modes and effects of Photoshop also work with text layers. Right-click the text layer, go down to Blending Options, and add a Drop Shadow, Outer Glow, or Stroke. Text remains in edit mode, so you can change your text and retain whatever effects have been applied to it.

Drawing Tools

The various drawing tools in Photoshop 2025 enable you to draw freehand elements, lines, and even more complex custom shapes to give you the ability to create artwork from scratch.

- **Brush Tool:** This is one of the most versatile tools, which allows hard and soft strokes depending on the type and opacity of the brush you have chosen. In Photoshop 2025, you can access more additional brush presets and will have improved control in the Brushes Settings panel over the brush dynamics, scattering, and flow.

- **Pen Tool:** The Pen Tool, under the shortcut P, is a tool used to draw correct and vector-based paths. You can make custom shapes, clip paths, or outlines with it. Photoshop 2025 has more advanced curve control (the Curvature Pen Tool), which allows you to draw smooth curves simply by clicking points, not dragging handles, making the use of this tool quite friendly for an end.

- **Pencil Tool:** Nested under the Brush Tool, the Pencil Tool is quite useful for roughing out sketches and pixel-based drawings. It is quite useful for projects like pixel art where you want the edges to be sharp.

- **Shape and Path Editing with the Direct Selection Tool**: Opening up the editing of a path or shape is done using the Direct Selection Tool, which allows access to the individual anchor points by using the key shortcut A. With this tool, you can fine-tune lines and curves. You can reshape any path by dragging its anchor points and control handles.

- **Customizable Brush and Pen Dynamics**: This feature allows more advanced configuration of pressure and tilt sensitivity in Photoshop 2025, which allows the use of a graphics tablet for an artist to gain greater control over brush flow and opacity due to pen pressure and tilt. This makes Photoshop an awesome tool for illustrators going after realistic drawing results.

Layer and Masking Techniques

Merging shapes, text, and drawing tools means that good layer management is imperative.

Here's how to make the most out of your layers in Photoshop.

- **Layer Masks**: Layer masks allow you to hide regions of a layer without actually deleting information. Mask text or shapes to enable fade and/or blended compositions. By using the Brush Tool on a layer mask, you can paint black to hide part of a layer or white to reveal it.

- **Clipping Masks**: Clipping masks help to constrain one layer inside the boundary of another. For example, you can add texture or any image to text by just adding a clipping mask over the text layer. Right-click the top layer and select **Create Clipping Mask**.

- **Smart Objects**: The shapes, text, and any other layers can be converted into Smart Objects that are always editable without including any damage. Preserves the data intact to apply filters or transformations without loss of quality of the original layer.

UNDERSTANDING FILE TYPES: PSD, JPEG, PNG, AND MORE

Like its predecessors, **Photoshop 2025** can support a wide array of file formats, each with different advantages and disadvantages depending on their intended uses. It will be helpful to know which file format should be used to ensure that the work is saved at the best quality possible and efficiently balanced in its file size, compatibility, and editability.

PSD - Photoshop Document

Features: PSD is the default file format native to Photoshop and is designed to store all the information of your work, including layers, masks, channels, and paths, along with all effects applied to that document via Photoshop.

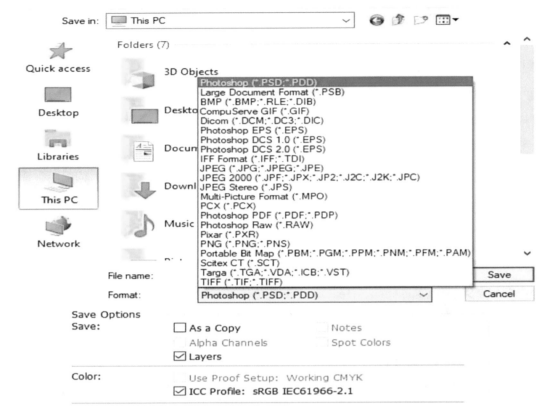

Advantages:

- **Editability**: The PSD file format retains all its layers and settings; hence, it is always editable. You can change something that is minute and tiny in it, but it never results in any quality loss.

- **High Quality**: PSD files are lossless, and no compression has been imposed on them, which means the details and colors remain just as exact as they were.

- **Maximum Compatibility within Adobe:** The PSD files merge seamlessly across all various applications of Adobe, including Illustrator, After Effects, and InDesign.

Disadvantages:

- **Large File Size**: Since PSDs are uncompressed and retain all their design elements, they can be rather large.

- **Limited Compatibility**: The PSD format is not compatible with just about any software or platform; they're mainly suited for use within the Adobe ecosystem or applications that support PSD.

Best Use Cases: PSD files are best used for projects that require heavy editing, such as ongoing design work, projects that will use layers, or when you need to share files with other designers for further collaboration.

JPEG (Joint Photographic Experts Group)

Features: JPEG probably stands out as one of the most frequently used image file formats in existence; it ensures great quality and isn't overly large, featuring lossy compression. A part of the data of the image is wasted, hence reducing the size.

Advantages

- **Light File Size**: Since JPEG is compressed, it means that JPEGs are ideal to be used on the web since they have small file sizes.

- **Highly Compatible:** The JPEG format is supported by all devices, applications, and browsers because of its very basic nature. Thus, it serves all purposes for most uses.

- **Adjustable Quality**: While saving, Photoshop gives an option to adjust JPEG quality, which comes in handy when it is necessary to balance the file size with the visual quality.

Disadvantages

- **Lossy Compression**: JPEG compression permanently discards some image information. The more a document has been changed and saved various times, the more one is losing in quality.

- **No Transparency Support:** JPEGs do not support transparency, making it inappropriate when images need transparent backgrounds.

Best Use Cases: JPEG is perfect for web images, social media content, and general-purpose photography in which maximum compression, along with compatibility on all platforms, is in focus rather than editability or minor details.

PNG (Portable Network Graphics)

Features: PNG allows for lossless compression, and transparency, and thus is one of the most commonly used web graphics, logos, and icons.

Advantages

- **Transparency**: PNG file formats have support for a transparent background, which makes them very useful in overlays, logos, and graphic elements over other pictures and backgrounds.

- **Lossless Compression**: PNG doesn't lose any quality of the image, so it is more suitable when retaining the original information is required

Disadvantages

- **Larger File Size Compared to JPEG**: As PNG is lossless compression file size will be greater as compared to JPEG. Therefore, it becomes less usable in web applications where file size is a major factor.

- **Not Ideal for Photographs**: Though excellent with graphics, PNG isn't usually used to capture photographs since it cannot compress the photo as well as JPEG.

Best Use Cases: PNG finds its perfect application in graphics, illustrations, logos, and web elements that require a transparent background or high information compression without heavy compression.

TIFF (Tagged Image File Format)

Features: TIFF is a lossless format and, therefore, maintains high-quality images; hence, it finds a place in professional printing and photography.

Advantages

- **Extremely High-Quality**: High-quality TIFFs retain all detail and are fit for high-resolution printing and professional editing.

- **Layer and Transparency Support**: Supporting layers and transparency, similar to PSD, are allowed when saving in TIFF with Photoshop, only in a more compatible format with other software.

Disadvantages

- **Very Large File Size**: Large files are difficult to share, download, and store. This is especially true if high resolution is applied.

- **Limited Web Compatibility**: Due to a lack of full-fledged compatibility, TIFF files are either used professionally or in offline mode.

Best Use Case: Professional photography, high-quality printing, and archiving images that need to retain all original data are some general uses of TIFF files.

GIF (Graphics Interchange Format)

Features: GIF is majorly known for support of animation and having small file sizes.

Advantages

- **Animation Support:** GIFs do support simple animation and, hence have been popular for small looping animations used in web content.

- **Small File Size:** GIFs are mostly small, hence easy to share and load on web pages.

Disadvantages

- **Limited Color Range:** GIFs only support 256 colors, making the images less vibrant and reducing quality for bigger and more complex images.

- **Not Ideal for High-Quality Images**: GIFS are best suited for carrying out the function of graphics, rather than high-detailed photographs or any kind of artwork.

Best Use Cases: GIFs work best in web animations, simple graphics, and meme content where depth and detail about color are not fundamental.

PDF (Portable Document Format)

Features: The PDF image file format is widely used for documents composed of images integrated with text. Most PDF documents come in multi-page format.

Advantages

- **Cross-Platform Compatibility**: PDFs can be opened on almost any device and hence are highly versatile in their shareability.

- **Preserves Image Quality:** PDFs retain high-quality images and preserve original formatting; great for print-ready documents.

Disadvantages

- **Less Ideal for Editing**: While you can import a PDF back into Photoshop for edits, PDFs aren't as editable as PSD files.

Best Use Cases: PDFs are best applied in final document presentations, portfolios, digital brochures, and print-ready files that merge images and text.

RAW (Camera Raw Formats)

Features: RAW files are uncompressed, minimally processed images taken from a camera's sensor and are best for photographers who will go deep into editing images.

Advantages

- **Maximum Quality and Flexibility**: Since the RAW files contain all the details, therefore, it offer maximum control during post-processing.

Disadvantages

- **Very Large File Sizes:** RAW files are big, and their format may also be different for different camera producers.

Best Use Case: It is suitable for professional photography, and advanced editing in Photoshop, where color correction requires the best quality.

CHAPTER FOUR

ADVANCED SELECTIONS AND MASKING

ADVANCED SELECTION TOOLS: OBJECT, QUICK, AND MAGIC WAND SELECTIONS

Object Selection Tool

The Object Selection tool has evolved, over time from its earlier versions in Photoshop, into one of the powerful means of selection with a set of new AI-driven enhancements in Photoshop 2025. Its power lies in identifying objects based on context, making it ideal for isolating elements such as people, animals, or objects that do not have tedious manual selections.

Using the Object Selection Tool

- **To Activate the Tool**: The Object Selection tool is nested with the Quick Selection tool inside the toolbar.

- **Making a Selection**: Click and drag either a rectangular or lasso area over an object you want to select. Photoshop will, by default, automatically detect and select the object within this defined area.

- **Refine a Selection**: After something has been selected, you can add to it, or take away from it. You can do this by hitting the **Shift** key to add, or the **Alt** key (Option on Mac) to take away.

Ideal Scenarios for the Object Selection Tool

- **Complex Background Subjects**: When one is working on a subject with a complex background, this tool easily separates the subject without much manual adjustment.

- **Creating Images for Composite Work**: This feature will see good application among designers who have to transfer elements from one background to another in a composite workflow.
- **Quick Isolation of Defined Objects:** While dealing with defined shapes, the Object Selection tool provides quick selection with one click.

Quick Selection Tool

The Quick Selection tool is arguably one of the most straightforward ways to make a selection, especially for those just starting to familiarize themselves with Photoshop. Similar to a paintbrush, you click and drag over an image; the similar tones and textures of that image will be detected in Photoshop as you drag the brush around, expanding the selected area as you go.

The Quick Selection Tool

- **Accessing the Tool:** The Quick Selection tool can be accessed via the toolbar; it is typically located in conjunction with the Object Selection tool.
- **Making Selections**: Using the brackets [ ] on your keyboard adjust your brush size then click and drag over an area you would like to select. Photoshopped instantly begins including adjacent areas of similar color and texture into your selection - automatically expanding the selection as you drag.
- **Fine Tuning with Add/Subtract Options**: Similar to the Object Selection tool, the Quick Selection tool gives you the option of adding or taking away from a selection. Holding Shift lets you add to it, while Alt allows you to subtract.

Ideal Scenarios for the Object Selection Tool

- **Editing Areas with Gradual Transitions**: This tool will work perfectly in cases when colors and textures change gradually, like skies, landscapes, or skin texture.
- **Quick Adjustments in Portraits**: In portrait editing, this quick selection tool will make it much easier to adjust some parts (for example, skin tone or hair color) and will enable the editor to perform more accurate adjustments.
- **Background Masking or Refinement:** This tool is especially effective in removing or changing the backgrounds of photos.

Magic Wand Tool

The Magic Wand tool is one of the oldest selection tools in Photoshop, yet it still holds its place within the workflow in Photoshop because of its somewhat different approach. This tool selects areas based on color and tonal range, whereas the other tools are context-aware.

This can be helpful when having a solid or consistent color, for example, in removing solid backgrounds or choosing areas of defined colors.

Using the Magic Wand Tool

- **Tool Implementation**: Locate the Magic Wand tool in the toolbar. It can be grouped with other select tools.

- **Make a Selection:** Click on a part of the image where you want to choose all neighboring pixels in a similar color range.

- **Adjusting Tolerance**: This Options bar setting determines the width of the color range this tool will select. A tolerance of 0 to 30 selects colors very similar to the clicked area, while a higher tolerance from 30 to 100 will include a broader range of tones.

- **Contiguous Option**: If the Contiguous is checked, the tool will pick only those pixels that are touching each other with similar colors. If unchecked, all the pixels of that color in the whole image will be selected.

Ideal Scenarios for the Object Selection Tool

- **Removing Simple Backgrounds**: This tool comes in handy for selecting carousing subjects from simple, solid-colored backgrounds. Consider the example of product shots on white backgrounds.

- **Working with Consistent Colors**: Should that area you need to select have a composition of colors that is consistent in tone (for instance, a logo or graphic element) the Magic Wand will work quite effectively.

- **Color-Based Selections:** Color-themed artwork in which the designer wants to isolate specific colors within a composition to easily adjust or replace those colors will find this tool helpful, i.e. Magic Wand.

AI-ENHANCED MASKING WITH SELECT AND MASK

Understanding AI-Enhanced Masking in Photoshop 2025

Masking gets a whole new dimension with Adobe Photoshop 2025, wherein it finally integrates AI right in the Select and Mask workspace. Algorithms powered by Adobe Sensei analyze each image to find fine details that normally require manual work: for example, tendrils of hair, thin fabrics, or generally complicated textures. This leads to faster, more precise, and intelligent selections, even for those images that have always given nightmare challenges.

Real-time feedback on the Select and Mask feature in Photoshop, powered by AI, enables users to make refinements and see instant changes.

AI drives better object recognition and edge detection, allowing the enhanced Select and Mask to identify complex subjects and backgrounds with high precision. Professionals and hobbyists alike save time while improving workflow efficiencies.

Improved Object Selection Tool with AI

The other great enhancement to the Select and Mask workspace in Photoshop 2025 is the AI-Enhanced Object Selection Tool. This will make selecting any object as easy as a single click, where the use of machine learning lets it differentiate between complex subject boundaries and recognize objects of any shape and texture. For example, if it works on an image of a model with flowing hair or of some product with a transparent background, then AI analyzes the composition and accounts for minute details by adjusting the selection boundary.

It's mainly good at subject isolation from busy backgrounds. Consider, for instance, the Object Selection Tool separating a tree with intricate branches or any other subject from a textured background without requiring extra work in refinement. With every interaction, it learns something new from Adobe Sensei, which further refines the capability with each update.

Refined Edge Detection with AI-Powered Smart Refinement

Photoshop 2025 refines the refinement of edges, and this is especially useful where there is hair, fur, or foliage in your selection. The new Smart Refinement, powered by AI, will automatically recognize the location of the edges and make the necessary adjustments. That means selecting a subject with complex textures of hair will be able to select individual strands of hair, refining the selection with a much more organic cutout that stitches together seamlessly into new backgrounds.

Besides all the Smart Refinement, Photoshop 2025 will also take care of colored contamination around selection edges. The AI algorithms detect color bleeding from the background and neutralize it to keep the natural tones of the selected subject. This saves time for artists who otherwise would need to go through steps of manual color correction after they have made their selection.

AI-Assisted Refine Mode: A Game Changer for Difficult Selections

Updates to features in Photoshop 2025 include an AI-Assisted Refine Mode that will allow the AI to work on highly complex images and come up with optimal settings regarding the detection of edges and refinement of selections. For example, if you are working on the image of a subject that is wearing some sort of semi-transparent veil, Refine Mode will capture not only the transparency of the fabric but also the subtle details beneath.

This will also enable "**smart brushing**" in which users can manually brush over areas, and the AI analyzes the stroked areas to understand where this selection needs more emphasis. Be it refining a mask for hair, smoke, or even reflections on water, Refine Mode ultimately helps artists get a high-quality selection with a lot less effort.

AI-Powered Background Removal Tool: Faster and More Accurate

With Photoshop 2025, it comes with an AI Background Removal Tool, which instantly and automatically separates a subject from its background. Unlike in older versions, this enhanced tool uses A.I. to perform the differentiation between foreground and background components in striking detail. The learning capabilities of Adobe Sensei make the tool handle even semi-transparent objects by automatically readjusting the selection to a clean, accurate cutout.

This Background Removal Tool is perfect for users interested in fast and efficient background removal, whether it be for e-commerce, portrait photography, or graphic design. Moreover, in just one click, separating the subject from the background will automatically have the AI adjust the mask to keep natural shadows and realistic contours.

Integrating AI-Based Object-Aware Brushes

Object-aware brushes have also been introduced into the Select and Mask workspace in Photoshop 2025. These brushes dynamically adjust to context, thanks to AI-powered detection of objects within a selection. Users can just brush along the edges of a subject; the sensitivity of the brush automatically adjusts as it does this to maintain a natural, precisely selected boundary.

For example, when over-painting a subject's hair and the background around it, the object-aware brush automatically detects subtle transitions between strands of hair and backgrounds and then refines the selection without requiring manual adjustment. In this way, this tool is perfect for artists working on detailed images, since it allows them to pay attention to creativity rather than spending time on technical refinements.

AI-Powered Mask Preview and Real-Time Adjustments

Photoshop 2025 offers the feature of real-time previewing of masks. While making any adjustments, the AI instantly gives feedback on an applied mask regarding how the edit is affecting the final output. The feature also further allows users to apply non-destructive adjustments directly within the workspace Select and Mask, in such a way that the changes can be tested without actually affecting the original image.

The real-time mask preview is a creation of actual value for any creative professional desiring selections to look as organic as possible. The feature also allows an artist to experiment with a variety of background scenarios and visual effects that include blending modes and layer styles right within the Select and Mask workspace without needing to exit it.

Effective Workflow Integration along with Enhancement of User Interface

With the addition of AI, this selects mask feature works together with other features in Photoshop, including Layers, Layer Masks, and Adjustment Layers. The update of 2025 makes this UI so intuitive that it's very easy to jump between tools. It cleaned up the workspace for all these AI-powered features, enabling users to do what they want in fewer steps.

Also, there's contextual help available now in the **Select and Mask workspace** that turns the **Tool Tips** ON by default. This, in essence, will walk a user through the new features while working. This should be particularly helpful for any beginners who might not quite understand AI-driven features, guiding them through the process and suggesting tools based on their actions.

REFINING EDGES FOR PRECISE SELECTIONS

Why Refine Edges?

Clean, accurate selections are the heart of digital compositing and image retouching in Photoshop, among a host of other workflows. Poor selections are prone to unnatural transitions between subjects and backgrounds, disrupting the realism and quality of the final image. Selection tools have been overhauled for 2025 in Photoshop, aiming at precision, efficiency, and ease with which difficult edges are tamed.

Selection Tools Overview: New and Enhanced

Photoshop 2025 also retains favorite selection tools, with modifications to increase ease when selecting and refining edges.

Quick Precursor Overview:

- **Quick Selection Tool:** This is improved with AI algorithms, making this tool faster and more accurate, perfect for larger selections.

- **Object Selection Tool**: It now recognizes and selects multiple objects within a scene, at times even pulling out backgrounds of subtly complex details.

- **Lasso Tools:** With ample practice in Photoshop tools, this also covers the polygonal and magnetic lasso used for controlling selection manually in a nonlinear fashion.

- **Magic Wand Tool:** Magic Wand Tool is ideal for selecting areas based on color and tone, and the improved edge detection now adapts to complex scenes.

Refine Edge Mode: A Deep Dive

Once you have made a selection, Refine Edge mode becomes your best friend. With the advanced algorithms in Refine Edge, Photoshop 2025 does particularly well with soft or jagged edges, such as hair, fur, and foliage.

Here's how you do it effectively:

1. **Refine Edge Access**: Once a selection has been made, go to the menu **Select > Select and Mask**. This opens the Refine Edge workspace where, at the top, options for View Mode, Edge Detection, and Global Refinements appear.

2. **View Mode Options**: Some options under View Mode in Photoshop 2025 include On Layers, Overlay, and Black & White, which allow for better visualization of your selection.

The black-and-white mode works great for detailed edges so that you can check where the soft or missed edges are.

3. **Edge Detection Tools:**

   - **Radius Slider:** Move the radius to capture finer details. A smaller radius works for hard edges while increasing the radius helps in processing soft and wispy textures.
   - **Smart Radius:** This setting works best for selections containing both hard and soft edges. For example, when trying to make a selection of a person, with both skin and hair in frame.

4. **Refine Edge Brush:** The Refine Edge brush will let you paint right over the edges to tell Photoshop where to include or exclude details. This is ideal for painting over areas such as hair so that it picks up stray strands or finer detail without affecting the selection as a whole.

Global Refinements: Fine-Tuning the Selection

In the Refine Edge workspace, you have options under Global Refinement to further enhance smoothness, feathering, contrast, and shifting of the edges:

- **Smooth**: This slider eliminates rough edges by softening them. This is ideal for selections that might seem choppy or jagged.

- **Feather**: You will add slight feathering; it gives the edge a slight blur, allowing you to integrate it with the new backgrounds effectively.

- **Contrast**: This slider increases the contrast along the edges, sharpening the selection boundaries; best for selections involving well-defined objects.

- **Shift Edge:** The edge can be shifted in or out. This will enable you to capture residual pixels along the edges.

With practice, these sliders will give you immense control over the appearance of the selection, allowing you to get the balance just right between smoothness and detail.

Hair and Fur Selection: Advanced Techniques

The tricky thing to select might be a texture, and that's where hair or fur comes in.

To make it easier, some new AI-powered enhancements have been added to Photoshop 2025:

- **Refine Hair Button:** This new tool is designed to analyze and refine selections of hair. Click the **Refine Hair button** within the Select and Mask workspace, and enable Photoshop to automatically adjust edge details to include stray strands without background interference.

- **Fine Tune with Overlay**: In the menu for View Mode, select **Overlay** and further adjust the opacity to see it better. Then, paint over the places where hair and fur strands merge with the background, as those are quite tricky and will be captured by the AI of Photoshop.

In very tricky areas, refine with both the Refine Edge Brush and the Refine Hair feature. That way, refinement for each area can be done according to the texture type, so it is accurate and seamless.

Refining Edges with the Masking Tool

Once you have made your selection, you can convert this into a layer mask and refine edges further by carrying out the following steps;

1. **Add a Mask:** Make sure the selection is active and click the **Add Layer Mask button** in the Layers panel - this will start concealing the background and preserving your selected subject.

2. **Refine with Brushes:** On the layer mask, a soft round brush will be used for manual cleaning of the edges. The opacity of the brush should be low to build up the adjustments to achieve subtle, natural-looking refinement.

3. **Using the Smudge Tool**: When it involves hair or any soft texture, the smudge tool will make very realistic softness on the mask edges and be very helpful when blending in a new background.

Outputting Your Selection

With Photoshop 2025, you can output the refined selections into various formats depending on how you would like your workflow to be:

- **Layer Mask**: This works best for non-destructive editing since you can refine the edges at any time.

- **New Layer with Mask**: A new layer is given with the selection in it, easing further adjustments without affecting the original.

- **New Document**: A new document export with a transparent background gives you a fresh canvas for composite work or additional design elements.

Each of these various output options will serve different purposes, so choose the one that best fits your project needs.

USING MASKING FOR NON-DESTRUCTIVE EDITING

Masking is a technique that allows one to screen or reveal selected parts of a layer or picture without actually deleting or changing the real image. The closest physical world analogy would be laying a semi-transparent sheet over an image and painting it black or white where you want to hide or reveal the picture beneath. In Photoshop, white areas on a mask are viewed, black areas are concealed, and shades of gray create partial transparency.

There are primarily two types of masks available in Photoshop:

1. **Layer Mask:** Applied directly to a layer to hide/reveal parts of the very same layer.

2. **Clipping Mask**: The content and transparency of one layer are used to control the visibility of another.

The Benefits of Non-Destructive Editing

Non-destructive editing implies that edits applied to an image do not affect the original pixels. Alternatively stated, at any moment in time, one can revisit work and alter, refine, or even eliminate edits created. Masking enables editors to:

- Edit parts of an image without permanently deleting any pixels.

- Apply effects or Adjustments to part of an image for testing.

- Easily refine edits to better suit a desired outcome.

This saves time, particularly in professional workflows where clients can demand changes at any time, or if one needs to reuse the asset for several projects using non-destructive methods such as masking.

Working with Layer Masks

Layer masks are the most common type of mask in Photoshop and are used for everything from basic corrections to complex compositing work.

Creating a Layer Mask

1. **Select Your Layer**: First, open your image and select the layer you want to mask.

2. **Add a Mask:** Finally, at the bottom of the Layers panel, click the **'Add Layer Mask'** icon (a rectangle with a circle in its middle).

3. **Paint on the Mask**: Once the mask is open, select the **Brush tool** and then select black as the Foreground Color of the mask to paint in some of the images. Then select white to return disappearing parts. Adjust the opacity and hardness of that brush to make subtle or harder effects.

The AI-powered Object Selection Tool, by default, automatically detects objects in Photoshop 2025, making selections quick and easy. This mask works with the tool to create initial selections for refined masking and saves time in complex compositions.

Refining a Layer Mask

1. **Feather and Density Adjustments:** Right-click the layer mask thumbnail and select **'Select and Mask'**. Here, you can feather the edges for a smooth merge, adjust the mask density to show and hide, and refine the mask in much greater detail.

2. **Edge Detection**: The new and improved Edge Detection algorithm in Photoshop 2025 (available inside the Select and Mask workspace) offers faster and more accurate refinement around the edges; very helpful when working with hair, fur, or complex textures.

Using Color Range and AI-Powered Selections

Adobe Photoshop 2025 has incorporated Adobe Sensei, which is the AI technology developed by Adobe, into its selection tools. You can now create masks based on Color Range and Object Recognition:

- **Color Range:** Go to **Select > Color Range** to create a mask based on particular colors within your image. It works well to isolate certain colors, like the sky or skin tone, for color adjustments.

- **AI-Powered Selections:** Instantly mask specific objects detected by Adobe's AI, such as people, animals, and buildings, by using the Object Selection Tool.

Using Clipping Masks

A Clipping Mask controls the visibility of one layer based on the contents of the layer below it. This becomes quite effective when placing a texture, color, or pattern on only a portion of the composite, but without having to make a complex selection against the entire image.

1. **Place Layers:** Put the layer you want to mask, such as a texture, above the base layer, which may contain text or a form.

2. **Create a Clipping Mask:** Right-click on the top layer and choose **'Create Clipping Mask'**. Thus, the content of the top layer is bound only within areas of the underlying layer that are not transparent.

Clipping masks are used throughout the world in digital artwork, where layers of textures, colors, or patterns are put together to gain depth and complexity in the art.

ADVANCED MASKING TECHNIQUES IN PHOTOSHOP 2025

Select Subject and AI-Driven Mask Refinement

The improved Select Subject tool in Photoshop 2025 instantly recognizes, while masking over persons, animals, and other main objects, a more accurate detection of predominant subjects in an image. This works very well with the Select and Mask workspace, where feathering can allow fine-tuning for smooth, clean edges.

Channel-Based Masking

Channel masking works wonders when the subjects are complex. It masks an image using its own RGB channels, depending on the tonal contrast of the image.

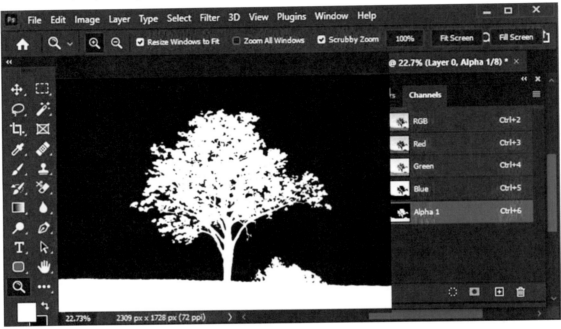

1. **Channel Selection**: In the Channels panel, select the channel with the maximum contrast between the subject and the background.

2. **Duplicating the Channel**: Right-click the channel selected, and duplicate it.

3. **Apply Adjustments**: Apply Levels or Curves to increase the contrast as much as possible, so that the subject becomes white and the background black.

4. **Load as Selection**: Ctrl + Click (or Cmd + Click) on the duplicated channel thumbnail to load it as a selection. Add this selection as a layer mask on your desired layer.

Channel masking is excellent when it comes to detailed areas like hair or smoke.

Vector Masks

Using Vector Masks in Photoshop 2025 has been improved and are vector editable with clean edges and are very well-suited to creating shapes and text. To create a vector mask, follow these steps:

1. **Add Shape Layer:** Draw a shape or write text using the Photoshop shape tool.

2. **Convert to Vector Mask:** With a right click on the shape or text layer, select **'Convert to Vector Mask'**. This gives you clear, sharp-edged masks that remain crisp even if resized.

Combining Masks for Advanced Editing

To get more complicated edits, combine masks on different layers to generate highly comprehensive, customized results:

1. **Apply Multiple Masks**: With Photoshop 2025, you are allowed to apply more than one mask on a single layer. Therefore, you can combine layer and vector masks or layer and clipping masks in one.

2. **Mask Multiple Layers**: Select multiple layers by grouping them using **Ctrl/Cmd + G**. Then apply a mask to this group. The technique of applying a mask to an entire group is great for a composition that involves multiple layers.

CHAPTER FIVE

IMAGE ADJUSTMENTS

APPLY A HUE/SATURATION ADJUSTMENT TO SELECTED OBJECTS

Hue/Saturation adjustment will be applied selectively to selected objects in Adobe Photoshop 2025 by the following steps, which are going to detail how to bring out the colors, tones, and vibrant effects that one may want.

Follow the steps below to apply a hue/saturation adjustment to selected objects:

Step 1: Open Your Image in Photoshop

- **Open Adobe Photoshop:** First, open Photoshop 2025 from your computer.
- **Open an Image**: Then go to **File > Open** and select the image you would like to work with.
- **Prepare Your Workspace**: Ensure you operate under **'Essentials'** by default so that all the panels you are going to need are open. To change it, head to **Window > Workspace > Essentials**.

Step 2: Select the Object(s) for Adjustment

1. Choose a Selection Tool: Choose any of the selection tools based on the shape and complication of the object by clicking on it from the toolbar. You can choose the Object Selection Tool, Quick Selection Tool, or Lasso Tool according to your needs.

- **Object Selection Tool:** This is quite a cool little tool that leans on AI to auto-detect and select objects. All you have to do is click and drag over the area you want to select, and in turn, Photoshop will outline it.

- **Quick Selection Tool**: If you have intricate shapes, then the Quick Selection Tool will enable you to click and drag within the object, which dynamically adjusts as you move to capture details.

- **Lasso Tool:** More precisely, the Lasso Tool will allow you to draw manually around the object.

2. Refine the Selection: Refined selection by using Select and Mask (available in the Options bar when object). Get refined edges of your selection with Smooth, Feather, Contrast, and Shift Edge options that give an appropriate selection.

Step 3: Apply a Hue/Saturation Adjustment Layer

1. Create an Adjustment Layer: With your object selected, enter the Layers Panel and click on the **Adjustment Layer icon** (the half-black, half-white circle). In the menu that comes up, choose **Hue/Saturation**.

Immediately, this adjustment layer will be applied only to your selected area, making a mask.

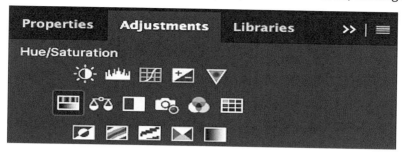

2. Understand the Hue/Saturation Panel: An essential Properties Panel appears for the Hue/Saturation adjustment. Three main sliders make up this panel:

- **Hue**: Alters the shade of color. It changes colors, moving the slider, within the selected area.

- **Saturation**: Changes the intensity of color. To increase the saturation, especially for bright colors, the slider should be moved to the right. To decrease the saturation, especially for pastel shades, the slider needs to be moved to the left.

- **Lightness**: Modifies the brightness. Colors will darken if the slider is moved to the left and lighten if moved to the right.

- **Adjust Colors Using Presets (Optional):** If you are attempting to create specific effects Sepia, Increase Reds, Desaturate, to name a few you can choose options under the presets menu in the three horizontal bars at the top right of the Properties Panel. On this menu, you can simply choose a preset to create a specific effect.

Step 4: Adjust the Hue Slider

1. **Adjust the Hue:** Move the Hue slider to either the left or right side, depending on what works best with your chosen object. You can try bringing small changes or slide it a little farther because all of the colors of the spectrum are covered under it for highly dramatic color changes.

2. **Edit in Specific Color Channels**: To make color changes to certain colors inside the selection, click the drop-down menu from which **'Master'** is displayed by default and select any of the color channels such as Reds, Yellows, Greens, etc. It gives more control to the individual colors inside the selected area.

3. **Observe Changes**: As you change the Hue, pay close attention to how that impacts your image in real time. Pay particular attention to areas with complex color gradients, as adjustments may affect different tones within your selection.

Step 5: Change Saturation and Lightness for the Preferred Effect

1. **Increase or Decrease Saturation**: The saturation slider will adjust your color values to become more vibrant or washed out. This will make objects pop if done slightly on colorful objects, such as flowers, while less saturation can give effects that are considered vintage or subdued.

2. **Adjust Lightness:** You can adjust the brightness of your selected area even more by using the Lightness slider. Lightning usually makes an object pop, whereas darkening is used to make it integrate better with the background.

3. **Combine Adjustments**: Often, small, gradual changes in the Hue, Saturation, and Lightness sliders yield the best results. Smaller, incremental adjustments will typically provide more natural results.

Step 6: Refine with the Layer Mask

1. Check the Layer Mask: You will notice that an adjustment layer has been created which includes a mask linked to your selection. This mask restricts the Hue / Saturation adjustment to only selected objects. If the selection wasn't perfect, you can now refine the mask.

2. **Paint on the Layer Mask**: Click the layer mask thumbnail to activate it, then select the Brush Tool and choose **Black** (over hides) or **White** (over reveals), and start painting over areas to refine the effect.

Use this to clean up edges and make sure the adjustment affects only the desired areas.

3. **Feather the Mask (Optional):** If the transition between adjusted and unadjusted areas seems too abrupt, then feather the mask. Double-click the layer mask thumbnail, and soften the edges using the Feather slider.

Step 7: Apply Blending Modes (Optional)

1. **Experiment with Blending Modes:** Once the Hue/Saturation layer has been chosen, in the Layers Panel experiment with blending modes (using the drop-down menu at the top of the list of layers). Some blending mode options, like Color or Soft Light, enhance or diffuse the adjustment to make even more creative possibilities for you.

2. **Opacity Adjustments**: Move the Opacity slider in the Layers Panel back off the adjustment. Less than 100% opacity may be all that's needed to get a more natural blend with the image around it.

Step 8: Final Adjustments and Saving

1. **Fine-tuning the Properties**: To further fine-tune the Hue, Saturation, or Lightness, go back into the Properties Panel. Make subtle changes to your ideal effect.

2. **Save Your Work**: Go to **File > Save As**, saving your image once all adjustments are to your liking. You will want this to be a PSD so it doesn't lose any layers when reopening in a later edit, or export it out as JPEG or PNG for the final use.

3. **Flatten the Image**: To have a one-layer image, go to **Layer > Flatten Image**. But remember first to save a copy with layers since this step cannot be undone.

USE THE REPLACE COLOR DIALOG

Here are the steps:

Step 1: Opening the Replace Color Dialog

1. **Open Photoshop and open your image**: First, open Adobe Photoshop 2025 and open the image in which you want to replace any color.

2. **Open Replace Color Dialog:** The **Image > Adjustments > Replace Color** opens the Replace Color dialogue window, which contains a host of color selection and adjustment controls.

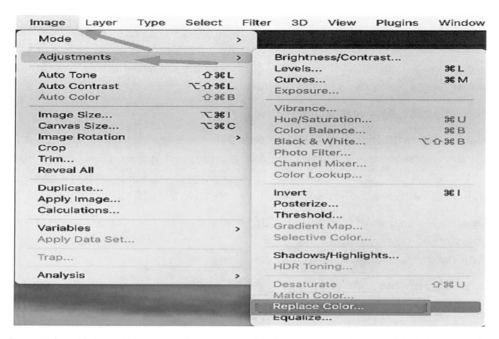

The Replace Color dialog allows you to change the hue, saturation, and brightness of selected colors in your image. This is convenient when you want to change colors but do not want to affect other areas.

Step 2: Select the Target Color

1. **Select Eyedropper Tool**: In the Replace Color dialog box, there are three eyedropper icons. The default Eyedropper tool is used to select a color; Add to Sample Eyedropper adds other areas of similar colors, while the **Subtract** from Sample Eyedropper removes parts from the selected color range.

2. **Click to Select Target Color:** Under the main Eyedropper tool, click on the part of the image that contains the color you want to replace. This selected color would then appear on the Replace Color panel in the Color Preview box and a black-and-white preview of the selection in the Mask Preview window.

3. **Move the Fuzziness Slider**: Below the Mask Preview, this determines the amount of the color range to include. A higher fuzziness will expand the color range, while a lower one contracts it. Move the slider to cover your desired area without affecting unintended sections.

Step 3: Fine-Tune the Selection (Optional)

1. **Use Add and Subtract Eyedroppers**: If the selected range of color does not spread over the target area completely, using the Add to Sample eyedropper click on different other areas until your selection spreads out.

If any areas that are not required are included, do the opposite: switch to the Subtract from Sample eyedropper and click to deselect them.

2. **Zoom in to be Precise:** Zoom into the image by using **Ctrl/Cmd + Plus**; this will help in selecting the precise areas. You might want to move around the image using Spacebar to make sure you include all areas of the target color and that you do not affect other parts of the image.

Step 4: Adjust the Replacement Color

1. **Adjust Hue, Saturation, and Lightness**: Below the Mask Preview window, you will see three sliders named Hue, Saturation, and Lightness. These sliders affect the characteristics of the replacement color.
   - **Hue**: This slider shifts the color to another hue. Assuming you are replacing red, by adjusting the hue, it could shift to blue, green, or any other hue.
   - **Saturation**: This slider decreases or increases the color's intensity. The color becomes more vibrant when moved towards the right and reduces when moved to the left.
   - **Lightness**: It affects the brightness of the color. When dragged to the right, the color brightens up while moving the slider on the left darkens it.

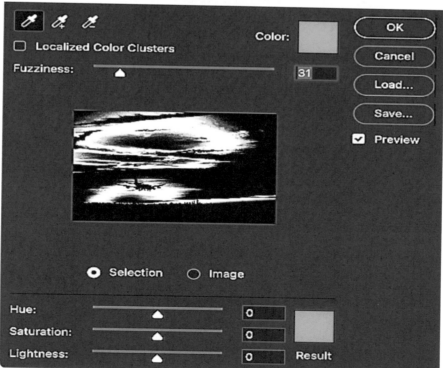

64

2. **Experiment with Settings**: Adjustments are usually small to achieve the results you want, so playing around with these sliders will get you the color. Suppose you wanted to change the color of that shirt from green to blue; you take the Hue slider and move it until you come onto a shade of blue, then work out Saturation and Lightness for a realistic feel, and you get your product.

Step 5: Preview and Before/After Comparison

1. **Check the Mask Preview:** While you are making an adjustment to these sliders, pay attention to the Mask Preview, which would ensure that only the desired parts get changed. You can turn the Mask Preview on and off by clicking the eye icon in the Replace Color dialog.

2. **Compare with Source Color:** For a quick before and after, select the Preview check box at the bottom left of the Replace Color dialog box. Select it and the image returns to its original colors, allowing you to make a side-by-side comparison with the source.

Step 6: Refine with Selections (Optional)

1. If some areas are not responding, well you may want to make a selection using one of the select tools, Quick Selection or Lasso for example, and contain the Replace Color adjustment to a selected area.
2. Make your selection, then open the **Replace Color dialog**.
3. Your adjustments will only be applied within the area you have selected, thus more control is achieved.

Step 7: Apply Changes

1. **Click OK:** When you feel that the color change is right, click OK to set the changes. The Replace Color dialog box is closed, and your changed color will be viewed in the main Photoshop window.

2. **Further Refinements**: If you need more changes, try adding the Hue/Saturation or Selective Color adjustment layers for finer adjustments of the replaced color.

Step 8: Save the Edited Image

- **Save Your Work**: Go to the File menu, click on **Save As**, choose the format your re-worked image is to be saved as - JPEG, PNG, etc. - then choose where you will save it. SAVE If you want to continue with further editing later on, it is recommended that you save a PSD format of your edited version so that the editable layers can be kept.

APPLY THE COLOR REPLACEMENT TOOL

The Color Replacement Tool is a strong option in Adobe Photoshop 2025 for users who need to change color in some of the elements that do not affect the image texture and details. It is quite useful during image overtones and enhancements in cases of color adjustment of clothes, backgrounds, or even object color concerning specific views.

Step 1: Open Your Image

- Open an image that you want to manipulate in Photoshop by going to **File > Open**, or just drag and drop it into the work area in Photoshop.
- If your image has several layers, ensure the layer you wish to change the color for is selected. Often, you'll want to be working on a duplicate layer - right-click the layer, and choose **Duplicate Layer**, so you can always go back to the original should you need to.

Step 2: Choose the Color Replacement Tool

- To open the Color Replacement Tool, click on and hold the icon of the Brush Tool or right-click on it, and choose **Color Replacement Tool** in the opened drop-down menu.
- You also can find it by pressing the **Shift+B** hotkey and cycling through all the brush-type tools.

Note: The Color Replacement Tool is hidden within the options of the Brush Tool, since it works similarly in that you paint over where you want to replace the color.

Step 3: Adjustments to Tool Settings

Before you begin to apply color, set up the tool appropriately.

Following are details about the major settings that you can play with:

1. **Brush Size**: Vary the size of the brush depending on the area you're coloring. You want a small brush for details, whereas you can go bigger for broader areas. You can change the size quickly by holding the [and] keys on your keyboard.

2. **Hardness:** This controls the hardness/softness of the edges of the brush. Lower values make for softer edges and are hence useful when one wants smooth transitions, while high values make for sharper edges.

3. **Sampling Options**:
   - **Continuous**: This samples colors continuously while painting, hence giving you the option of replacing several colors across the area.
   - **Once**: It samples the color once upon starting to paint and gives you the option of changing it with only the first selected color.
   - **Background Swatch:** Replaces only those parts that correspond to the background color as defined in the color palette.

4. **Limits**:
   - **Contiguous**: Affects only adjacent pixels and thus can retain colors within certain boundaries. This is effective for more precise coloring.
   - **Discontiguous**: Affects all similar colors within the range of the brush, even when not connected. It works well on larger surfaces without interference.
   - **Find Edges:** Preserves the edges of objects, helping in giving a real look and changing only the interior color.

5. **Threshold**: Keep deciding how similar the colors you're painting over Photoshop matches. If the tolerance is low, the tool is restricted to colors that are close to your sampled color, while if the tolerance is high, then a wider range of colors gets changed.

Step 4: Select New Color

- **Next**, you need to specify a replacement color. Do that by choosing your foreground color via the Color Picker. For the **Color Picker dialog** to pop up, click on the foreground color in the toolbar.
- Once the Color Picker dialog opens, either choose your color or create/input an exact hex code if needed for precise color matching.
- It is better to blend colors when the tone needs a complementary color with the original tones of the image, especially over complicated textures or lighting.

Step 5: Begin Painting Over the Area

- Now, click and drag the brush across the area in which you want to apply the new color. Sweep the brush right over the area you want to recolor, following any edges and contours.
- If you are working on an image with a lot of details, you should zoom in for precision. You can do this by pressing **Ctrl +.**
- Make sure that you use a smaller brush size and also have a lower tolerance during detailed work on small areas.

Step 6: Adjust Blending Mode (Optional)

For even more flexibility, try adjusting blending modes. These controls, located in the options bar at the top, define how the new color will interact with the original pixels.

Popular choices include:

- **Color**: Applies the color only, and doesn't affect the grayscale underneath for realistic color changes.

- **Hue**: Affects hue only and doesn't change the saturation and value of the original.

- **Saturation**: Only changes saturation, not hue and brightness set previously Each option of a blending mode provides an effect that can be very distinct; therefore, you may want to experiment to decide what looks good for your image.

Step 7: Sharpen the Edges

- **Finally**, with the color applied, you will often find that the edges of an area are a little rough or could be better refined. This is easy to clean off any extraneous color that may have spilled out of its intended area by making use of the Eraser Tool.
- If your color change is too jarring, then try reducing the opacity of the Color Replacement Tool for a softer blend with the old color.
- **Alternatively**, one may use a Layer Mask with the duplicated layer for more control; one would paint the color on the mask for a non-destructive edit of **'painting in'.** This enables one to erase or adjust those areas easily.

Step 8: Review and Make Final Adjustments

- Once the color replacement is satisfying, zoom out to see an overview of the image. Check for any spots you might have overlooked and make further enhancements.
- You can also fine-tune the brightness/contrast or hue/saturation to perfect the look of your new color.

Step 9: Save Your Edited Image

- Once your color replacement is how you want it, save your work by going to **File > Save As** and choosing your preferred format. For layered, editable files, save as a PSD.
- If you're ready to share or go to print, choose a compressed format like **JPEG** or **PNG**.
- Save your project in a high-quality format to retain details in color, especially when printing the image or using it commercially.

PREVIEW AND APPLY MULTIPLE BLUR TRACES

Check the steps below:

Step 1: Open Your Image and Access the Blur Gallery

1. Open Photoshop and open any image you'd want to work on.

2. With an image opened, click on the top navigation bar where it says **Filter**.

3. Look down the menu for **Blur Gallery** and click to reveal options like Field Blur, Iris Blur, Tilt-Shift, and the newest of all, Path Blur for motion effects.

4. Click on **Path Blur** to enable the Blur Gallery interface where you will work with several blur traces.

Step 2: Understanding Blur Traces

1. Before applying multiple blur traces, let's understand what a blur trace is in Photoshop 2025. Blur traces are the paths along which you create custom blur effects that define the direction and intensity of the blur.

2. Each trace can simulate motion in a specified direction, mimicking effects like car movement, wind, or subject speed. The Blur Gallery has added the ability to add multiple blur traces, each with unique directions and intensities.

Step 3: Add Your First Blur Trace

1. Locate the **Add Path button** in the Path Blur panel and click it to start drawing your blur trace directly onto the image.

2. With the cursor, draw a line across the part of the image where the motion blur should occur. Continuing with the previous example of an image of a runner, draw the blur trace along the path of the runner.

3. Once you have drawn the line, you will notice that control points have appeared at either end. These control points enable you to adjust the direction and length of the blur. You could click and drag these points to further refine the path of the blur trace.

4. Back in the **Path Blur options**, adjust the **Speed** to determine how much blur there is on this trace.

Step 4: Preview the First Blur

- With the first blur trace, you begin to instantly enable a preview of the applied effect view in Photoshop 2025.
- This is a live preview for accurate determination of how the motion blur has affected your image. Refined by adjusting the control points, speed, or direction.

Step 5: Add Multiple Blur Traces

1. Click on the **Add Path button** to add another blur trace.

2. Create the new blur trace in a position where you want to add more motion. For example, if you are editing a cityscape in which you would like multiple cars to have a separate motion, you can create a blur trace for every car along the path of each one.

3. Each trace can have its unique direction, speed, and intensity to let you make complex scenes with variant motion effects.

Step 6: Editing Individual Blur Traces

1. Click anywhere on the Blur Gallery workspace to enable the blur trace.

2. **Traces are independent of one another, and their settings can be adjusted as follows:**

   - **Direction**: Move the handles to adjust the angle of the blur so it matches the object's intended movement.
   - **Speed**: Use the speed slider to increase or decrease the strength of the blur on this particular path.
   - **Taper**: This option lets you fade out the blur trace naturally around the edges to give a realistic feel to the motion of the object in the picture.

3. Refine each trace further by playing with the Effects panel available under Path Blur, where you get options to control parameters such as Strobe Strength and Strobe Flashes for creating staccato-like blur effects simulating a succession of movements in quick succession - best suited for fast-action shots.

Step 7: Comparing Blur Traces

Photoshop 2025 A new panel, Preview Panel, lets one compare how each blur trace is affecting the shot individually. This comes in useful in the case of multiple blur traces because you enable the view of one trace at a time, and notice how each adds to the final result.

- Click the eye icon next to each blur trace to toggle it on and off.

- Use the **Preview Panel** to see the impact of each blur trace or select them all to get the overall merged effect.

Step 8: Fine-Tune with Smart Filter Options

Since Photoshop 2025 supports Smart Filters, you can apply non-destructive blur traces to your image.

1. The layer has to be converted to a Smart Object first to access the Blur Gallery, in such a way that all the blur effects are not destructive and can be edited later.

2. Once you have added several blur traces, you need to go back into the Blur Gallery for any edits on every single trace that does not affect the other parts of your image.

3. You can put a layer mask on your Smart Filter, also allowing selective blurring within the layer.

Step 9: Save and Export

Once you are satisfied with your multiple blur traces:

1. Click **OK** in Blur Gallery to apply the effects.

2. If you are working with multiple layers or Smart Filters, you will save your file in the PSD format to preserve layers and allow future edits.

3. For final output, go to **File > Export > Export As** and save your image in your desired format - JPEG, PNG, among others.

SHARPEN USING SMART SHARPEN

The steps:

Step 1: Open Your Image and Duplicate the Layer

1. Open Photoshop 2025 and open your image.

2. Click on the top banner, select **File > Open,** and find your image.

3. With this duplicate layer, you will avoid edits to the original image. To do this, click on the **Background layer**, right-click to pull up more options, click on **Duplicate Layer**, or press **Ctrl + J** for Windows or **Cmd + J** for Mac.

4. Immediately, rename the duplicated layer to "**Sharpened**" or something of that sort, just so you can switch between the original and sharpened layers to get an idea of how you're coming along.

Step 2: Apply the Smart Sharpen Filter

1. Keep your duplicated layer active.

2. Navigate to **Filter > Sharpen > Smart Sharpen**.

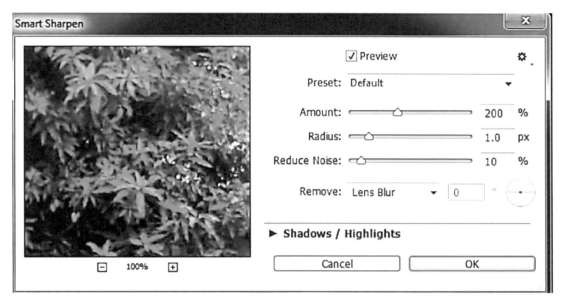

3. A Smart Sharpen dialogue box opens showing a preview window with various editable options to fine-tune the sharpen effect.

Step 3: Understanding the Smart Sharpen Settings

In the Smart Sharpen dialog, you will have the following settings:

- **Amount**: Controls the intensity of sharpening. A larger amount gives more pronounced edges but may add a little noise if this exceeds.

- **Radius**: It decides the width of the sharpening effect. Higher radius values can lead to haloing-visible outlines around objects. So, only adjust with care.

- **Reduce Noise**: This option reduces the noise that sometimes may occur with sharpening. It's pretty useful for high-ISO images or those images that contain grain.

Besides that, there are Shadow and Highlight options that give you the ability to control the dark and light areas so that the sharpening effect will not be overexposed in any area of the tone.

Step 4: Set the Amount and Radius

1. Originally, the Amount can be set at around **100%**. Then, it can be increased or decreased depending on your image's need for sharpness.

2. Adjust the **Radius** depending on the resolution and detail in your image. You more often than not get away with a Radius of 1.5 to 3 pixels for high-resolution images while a smaller image may only need 0.5 to 1 pixel.

3. View the image in the preview window while adjusting Amount and Radius. You can use the plus and minus icons on the preview window to zoom in/out for an even closer view of image details.

Step 5: Noise Reduction

- Sharpening sometimes amplifies noise, particularly in low-light images. To counter this, use the Reduce Noise slider.
- Increase and Reduce Noise gradually until the unwanted noise is minimized without softening the important details. You want a balance that will sharpen the edges but keep the image clean.

Step 6: Fine-Tune Shadows and Highlights

1. **Shadow and Highlight -** These two settings let you adjust the sharpening amount separately for the darker and lighter regions of the image. This will help in not over-enhancing too bright or dark regions.
2. **Advanced Mode -** This box should be checked if you want to see shadow and highlight controls individually.
3. If the dark areas appear to be too sharp or noisy, adjust the **Fade Amount slider** for **Shadows**. Similarly, to reduce sharpening in the bright areas, adjust the Highlight Fade slider.
4. Further, adjust the **Shadows** and **Highlights** sliders of Tonal Width and Radius for a balanced effect.

Step 7: Preview the Results

1. Check and uncheck the **Preview checkbox** to view your changes on the image.
2. This will allow you to compare side by side the original and sharpened versions to determine if further adjustments will be needed.

Step 8: Apply Smart Sharpen Filter

1. Click **OK** when you are satisfied with your settings to apply the Smart Sharpen effect on your duplicated layer.
2. Allow the changes to process, and eventually, Photoshop will return you to your main workspace with your sharpened image layer set.

Step 9: Refine with Layer Mask (Optional)

1. If some areas of the picture seem too sharp, you can add a Layer Mask to the sharpened layer.
2. Now go to the "**Sharpened**" layer and click the icon at the bottom of the Layers panel for the Layer Mask.

3. Take a soft brush with low opacity and start painting over the area where you want the sharpening to be less evident; thus, sharpening will be selective only in places that you choose.

Step 10: Check and Save Your Work

1. When satisfied, check the final effect of turning the sharpened layer on and off.

2. When all is in order, go to F**ile > Save As**, and choose your file format - JPEG, PNG, or PSD if you want to keep the layers.

3. For this, save under a new filename to keep both an original and edited copy.

BLUR IMAGE AREAS

Follow the steps below:

Step 1: Open the Image in Adobe Photoshop 2025

1. **Launch Photoshop**: Launch Adobe Photoshop 2025 from your computer.

2. **Open Your Image:** Once the program opens, click on **File > Open**, then select the image file that you want to work on. Highlight the image and select **Open**. This will load the image into your workspace.

Step 2: Duplicate the Layer

1. **Create a Backup Layer:** Since a little error may be an irritant, one should always create a backup layer on which one is operating, and that can always be returned if need be.

2. **Duplicate Layer**: Right-click the image layer, often labeled as "**Background**," inside the Layers panel and select from the menu options, click **Duplicate Layer**. The new layer opened will be used in applying the blur effect.

Step 3: Select What to Blur

1. **Use a Selection Tool**: Based on the area you want to blur, select a selection tool that works well for that part.
   - **Rectangular Marquee Tool**: Basically, create a rectangular or square selection.
   - **Elliptical Marquee Tool**: When you want to choose something that is a circle or oval in shape.
   - **Lasso Tool**: For free-form selections. Just trace around the part of the image you would like to blur.
   - **Quick Selection or Magic Wand Tool**: You will not have to do anything, as the tool will make selections automatically because it will note color and texture similarities.

2. **Refine Selection Edge:**
   - Feather your selection, via the Feather option in the Options Bar at the top, to make the edges soft so the blur will subtly merge into unblurred portions of the image. A feather radius of 10-20 pixels works usually but is dependent on image size and resolution.

Step 4: Blur the Selection

1. **Open the Filter Menu**: Keep the selected area active and then go up to the top menu to **Filter > Blur**. There are several different blur options available within Photoshop, so choose one now that best suits the style of the effect you're trying to achieve.
   - **Gaussian Blur:** A soft, general-purpose blur. It works great for subtle blurs or making something a background blur.
   - **Lens Blur**: It emulates the depth-of-field effect from camera lenses. Perfect for blurring backgrounds and leaving the foreground sharp.
   - **Motion Blur:** This applies a blur in a specific direction, which is useful when you want to create the effect of movement or speed.
   - **Field Blur:** This allows you to decide on the strength of the blur by placing multiple points on the image, and choosing their blur strength.

2. **Blur Strength Adjustment**:
   - Each type of blur filter has its adjustment settings. For example, with Gaussian Blur, you will get a slider to adjust the Radius. The blur grows stronger with an increase in radius.
   - For Lens Blur, you can adjust the **Radius**, **Blade Curvature**, and **Rotation** to achieve the desired look of the blur.

3. **Preview Effect**: For most of the blur options, you will see an option for a live preview. Use the sliders while seeing how the blur interacts with the selected area in your image. When satisfied with it, click **OK** to apply the blur.

Step 5: Refine the Edges

1. **Deselect and Check:** Once blurred, go to **Select > Deselect,** or use the keyboard shortcut **Ctrl+D for Windows/Cmd+D for Mac**, to discard the selection. Check the blurred portion to see that it merges naturally with the rest of the image.

2. **Use Layer Masks for Precision**:
   - To soften any coarse or abrupt blur you'll be dealing with the layer masks. Make sure the blurred layer is active and click the **Add Layer Mask icon** at the bottom of the Layers panel.

- Choose the **Brush Tool** and select a soft round brush. Ensure the Foreground Color is black (black conceals, white reveals). The painting around the edges of the blurred area softly blends with the surrounding image.

Step 6: Add More Blur Effects if Needed

1. **Multiplicity of Blur Layers**: If your image has several areas with priorities for different blurring, duplicate the layer. Always start afresh when beginning a new area.

   This would ensure different blurs in different areas without interference.

2. **Use Smart Filters to Gain Flexibility**:

   - First, convert the layer to a Smart Object in advance of the blur effects. Right-click on the layer and then select **Convert to Smart Object**.
   - Now, any blur you apply will be added as a Smart Filter under the layer. This will allow you to go back and adjust the blur strength or type at any time by double-clicking the filter in the Layers panel.

Step 7: Fine-Tune and Merge Layers

1. **Fine-Tune Blurred Areas**: You have the option to make minor adjustments in the blur strength if it's needed. With Smart Filters, you can make these changes easily by re-accessing the filter settings.

2. **Merge Layers (Optional):** Once you feel satisfied with the effect, you can merge all layers into one to finalize your image.

   Just go to **Layer > Merge Visible**, or press Ctrl+Shift+E for Windows/Cmd+Shift+E for Mac to combine it into one single layer; however, keep it on different layers in case at some point you feel like you want to adjust some areas.

Step 8: Save Your Work

1. **Save as Photoshop Format:** This will keep the layers and edits intact; hence, you should save a copy of your work in Photoshop natively in its **.PSD format**.

   Go to **File > Save As** and choose Photoshop (*.PSD). That way, you'll have the chance to reopen the file later and make further changes.

2. **Export for Use**: If you want the image in another format, say JPEG or PNG, go to **File > Export > Export As**. Choose your format, quality, and resolution settings to your liking, and click Export.

BEFORE MAKING COLOR AND TONAL ADJUSTMENTS

Approaching color and tonal adjustments in Adobe Photoshop 2025 should be done methodically. Proper preparation will provide accurate, consistent, and aesthetically pleasing results.

Step 1: Understand Your Image and Set Goals

Analyze the Image

- Start by carefully evaluating the image for color and tone needs. Does this image need color correction to eliminate color casts? Does this image need a tonal correction to reveal details in either shadows or highlights?
- Identify what you want to enhance or correct in the image and define a visual goal. These will help guide the rest of your workflow and help you make precise adjustments.

Evaluate Lighting Conditions

- Consider the environment in which the photo was taken and how it affects color and tone. Images taken in natural light may require different adjustments compared to those shot under artificial light.
- Familiarity with how light sources affect color and tone will help you make informed choices about what the image needs.

Step 2: Calibrate Your Monitor

Why Calibration Matters?

- Correct color management requires a well-calibrated monitor. Calibration will ensure the colors you see on your screen are the same as those in the image file.
- If your monitor isn't calibrated, you run the risk of colors and skin tones appearing different on another screen or in print.

Hardware and Software Calibration

- Use physical hardware to help in color calibration, like a colorimeter, or dedicated software that will step through adjusting brightness, contrast, and color tones on the monitor.
- There are a number available. For monitors, they may come with included built-in tools like **Dell UltrasSharp** or third-party software such as **X-Rite** or **Datacolor**. Naturally, frequently performing the calibration monthly will help achieve a cohesive set of ideal results.

Step 3: Set Up the Workspace

Configure Photoshop Workspace

- The new options to customize the workspace appear in Adobe Photoshop 2025. Now select the workspace layout, which will be best suited for color and tonal adjustments.
- In Photoshop, choose **Window > Workspace > Photography** to access most of the tools used in photo editing. This panel customization lets you get control over color, histogram, layers, and properties.

Choose the Right Color Settings

- Open color settings via **Edit > Color Settings**. Now select a color working space, in RGB, of course. For most digital work, sRGB is just fine. It will ensure a complete web display.
- If you are printing, then **Adobe RGB or ProPhoto RGB** might serve you better. They house a broader range of colors.

Step 4: Work Non-Destructively

Using Adjustment Layers

- The great thing about adjustment layers is that edits can be performed non-destructively. To create an adjustment layer, select **Layer > New Adjustment Layer** and choose from options under **Curves, Levels**, and **Hue/Saturation**.
- The beauty of adjustment layers is that they can be turned on and off, modified, or deleted at any time because they will never permanently affect the original image.

Use Smart Objects

- Smart Objects allow for filters and adjustments to be applied nondestructively. To make a layer into a Smart Object, right-click on the layer and select **Convert to Smart Object**.
- When you work with Smart Objects, the original information is maintained since editing adjustments are easier without loss of quality.

Step 5: Assess Histogram and Image Data

Read Histogram for Tonal Information

- The histogram is the graphical representation of your image's brightness values. Opening the histogram panel can be found under **Window > Histogram**. The left side corresponds to shadows, middle to mid-tones, while the right side corresponds to highlights.
- A well-balanced histogram would usually indicate that the image is well exposed, but data bunched on either side may indicate some under- or overexposure.

Check Shadow and Highlight Clipping

- The clipping shows the pixel as either pure black or pure white without any detail. Pressing and holding the **Alt** key on Windows, or the **Option** key on Mac, while adjusting sliders in Levels and Curves adjustments will show areas of the image that have clipped.

- This is an excellent way to precisely know where clipping will occur so you can hold onto those highlights and shadows.

Step 6: Assess and Refine Color Casts

View Color Casts

- Color casts exist when an image possesses an unwanted tint. To find a color cast, select **Layer > New Adjustment Layer > Threshold** and use a **Threshold Adjustment Layer.** Using this layer determine the pure white and pure black points. Sample those points with the Eyedropper Tool, which will help to set the neutral color balance.

Correct Color Casts

- Having found color casts, correct them with Color Balance (**Image > Adjustments > Color Balance**) or the Curves adjustment layer. Apply Auto Color for quick fixes, but to create more natural-looking images you must make manual adjustments to balance the colors of the image.

Step 7: Basic Global Adjustments

Exposure and Contrast

- A well-exposed image is the foundation of all subsequent color and tonal adjustments. Start with either the Levels or Curves adjustment layer.
- In Levels, move the black and white sliders inward to increase the contrast by darkening the shadows and lightening the highlights. You can create an S curve in Curves that will enhance the contrast yet maintain detail.

Use Vibrance and Saturation Sparingly

- When saturating/enhancing colors use Vibrance before Saturation to avoid over-saturating already brightly colored areas.
- Vibrance will boost the intensity of more muted colors while also considering skin tones. To adjust: **Layer > New Adjustment Layer > Vibrance**. Go in gradual increases to keep the image natural.

Step 8: Check and Make Selective Adjustments

Selective Color and Tone Adjustments

- Sometimes you want to impact only part of an image with color or tone. Masks allow you to make selections for adjustments. For instance, you can add a mask to an adjustment layer.
- Then you can use a soft brush to paint areas of the mask with black to hide those areas of the adjustment so you can make localized color or tone refinement.

Use Hue/Saturation for Targeted Adjustments

- The Hue/Saturation adjustment layer allows you to make specific color adjustments to the various color channels.
- This tool is great for adjusting selected colors within an image. For example, if a sky looks too cyan, you can adjust the cyan slider to find a more natural color tone.

Step 9: Double-Checking and Finalize Adjustments

Zoom In and Out

- Before making all the final adjustments, zoom in to check the details and zoom out to see the effect of the adjustment on the image as a whole.
- Sometimes an adjustment can introduce artifacts or unduly exaggerate the tones, such as banding in a gradient or halo effects around the edges.

Compare Before and After

- To see the overall impact of your edits, turn the view for each of your adjustment layers on and off.
- By flipping between before and after, you'll be better able to judge your edits and make any final alterations.

Save and Document Edits

- Once satisfied with the color-adjusted image, save it in a format that supports layers such as PSD or TIFF. This keeps all of the layers intact for later modification.
- If the images are several in number, document the process of adjustment or create a Photoshop action to maintain consistency throughout multiple edits.

MAKE A COLOR ADJUSTMENT

Color Adjustment in Adobe Photoshop 2025: This is the step-by-step process one ought to consider in ensuring that there is comprehensive and detailed enhancement of images. Color adjustment in photo editing involves the correction and creative manipulations of color tone, contrast, and saturation to achieve the desired appearance of an image.

Step 1: Open Your Image in Adobe Photoshop 2025

1. **Launch Adobe Photoshop 2025**: Open the application and enter your workspace. Ensure that your workspace layout is "**Photography**" in case edits are being done on photos only, which may have great convenience with adjustment tools.

2. **Load Your Image:** Open **File > Open**, and then load your image. You should see it loaded onto the main canvas with the Layers panel to the right.

Step 2: Create a Duplicate Layer (Optional but Recommended)

The reason you work on a duplicate layer is so edits can be made non-destructively.

1. **Duplicate the Layer**: Right-click on the background layer in the Layers panel and select Duplicate Layer, or use the quick way by pressing Ctrl + J for Windows or Cmd + J for Mac.

2. **Rename the New Layer (Optional):** Rename the new layer's name by double-clicking on it and perhaps calling it "**Color Adjustments**." That helps you know what you did if you make any edits.

Step 3: Access Color Adjustment Tools

There are numerous ways through which color adjustments can be done in Photoshop. The two major methods through which this is done include Image Adjustments and Adjustment Layers.

1. **Image Adjustments:** This is done by going to **Image > Adjustments.** Changes made through this method are directly on the layer. Therefore, since it affects the layer directly, adjustments are destructive since they change the pixels permanently.

2. **Adjustment Layers:** This is recommended. The **Adjustment Layer icon** is located at the bottom of the Layers panel and consists of a half-black and half-white circle. It will give you non-destructive editing, meaning you can go back later and change settings without affecting the original image.

Step 4: Determine the Color Adjustment Type

There are numerous color adjustment options available in Adobe Photoshop 2025, providing adjustments for brightness, contrast, saturation, and color tones.

Brightness/Contrast

1. **Add a Brightness/Contrast Adjustment Layer**: Click the **Adjustment Layer icon** and select **Brightness/Contrast.** This is a global adjustment that works great for making any correction in the overall exposure.

2. **Move the Sliders:** The Brightness slider will lighten or darken the image and the Contrast slider increases or decreases contrast. Note in your image what effect this has as you make your change.

Levels

1. **Add a Levels Layer**: Click the **Adjustment Layer icon** and select Levels. In this tool, you will be able to work on the adjustment of the shadows, midtones, and highlights.

2. **Understand the Histogram**: Levels histogram will show the tonal range of an image. Shadows will be at the left, midtones in the middle, and highlights at the right.

3. **Move the Sliders**: Drag the black, gray, and white sliders beneath the histogram to set the intensity for the shadows, midtones, and highlights, respectively.

Curves

1. **Add a Curves Layer**: The menu option opens the Curves adjustment layer: **Adjustment Layer > Curves.** The major strength of Curves is its value as an accurate, fine-grained brightness and contrast controller.

2. **Move the Curve Line:** The diagonal line represents the tonal range. To put it another way, you click the line to set anchor points and drag them upward or down, lightening or darkening parts of the tonal range.

3. **Adjust Specific Channels**: By default, the dropdown menu will be set to RGB, but this can be changed to allow for single color channel adjustments of Red, Green, and Blue for selective color balancing.

Hue/Saturation

1. **Insert Hue/Saturation Layer**: Create through **Adjustment Layer > Hue/Saturation**. You can change the colors one by one here by adjusting hue, saturation, and lightness.

2. **Change Master Colors:** Drag the hue to change the color, Saturation to increase or decrease the intensity of the color, and Lightness to lighten the color or make it darker.

3. **Selective Color Range:** Use this menu to select a specific color range like Reds, Greens, or Blues to make fine color adjustments.

Color Balance

1. **Color Balance Layer:** Create an adjustment layer by going to **Adjustment Layer > Color Balance**. This works well in color cast correction.

2. **Adjust Midtones, Shadows, and Highlights:** After selecting one of these three major tonal ranges that you would like to change, move the Cyan/Red, Magenta/Green, and Yellow/Blue sliders until the color balance is achieved.

Step 5: Apply Adjustments Selectively by using Masks

By default, an adjustment layer will also include a mask, which enables you to target color adjustments for only specific regions of the image.

1. **Click the Mask**: In the Layers panel click on the white box (mask) to the right of your adjustment layer.

2. **Using the Brush Tool**: Having selected the Brush Tool, with black as its color, you simply have to paint over an area where they do not want the adjustment to be applied, and it will be masked there.

3. **Refine Edges:** Using a soft-edged brush, feather your adjustment in smoothly with the rest of the image.

Step 6: Experiment with Blending Modes (Optional)

Blending modes control how the adjustment layer interacts with the underlying layers.

1. **Choose Blending Mode**: To choose a blending mode in the Layers panel, click the Blending Mode drop-down menu; this will default to Normal. Now, either Multiply, Screen, or Overlay mode will give you that different feel.

2. **Adjust Layer Opacity:** Another quick way is to lessen the impact of your adjustment layer by clicking on the Opacity drop-down menu.

Step 7: Fine-Tuning the Adjustment Layers

Sometimes, for things to work best, you may want to toggle among multiple adjustment layers, setting them just right. To get the best results, you may need to go back and forth between a few adjustment layers.

1. **Double-Click the Adjustment Layer Icon**: If you double-click an adjustment layer icon (the Brightness/Contrast icon). For instance, you can reopen its adjustment settings and then adjust the values.

2. **Add Multiple Adjustments**: You can make several adjustment layers; one after another, like Hue/Saturation followed by Curves, for example, to create an elaborate color correction.

Step 8: Review and Save Your Work

1. **Check the Image**: Switch on and off different adjustment layers by clicking the eye icon before each layer to show before-and-after comparisons.

2. **Save Your Document**: Save your document in PSD format to save the layers for further editing; for export, go to **File > Export > Export As**, and select a format such as JPEG or PNG.

Step 9: Experiment with Presets (Optional)

Presets provide instant color corrections and can be particularly useful if you are a novice working with colors in Photoshop 2025. **To begin with a preset:**

1. **Select Preset**: With any of the adjustment layers, such as Curves or Hue/Saturation, most adjustment menus have a preset selector. Sometimes, it might be helpful to use one as the place to begin.

2. **Make Fine Adjustments:** Some of the presets will permit further modification to provide a customized adjustment.

Step 10: Save Your Custom Adjustments Option

- **Save a new preset:** after changing some or all the settings, click the **Save button** at the top of the Adjustments panel and save your settings as a preset. Later on in another project, you can apply the same adjustment settings to another photo and it saves you time.

HOW TO CROP AND STRAIGHTEN PHOTOS

Step 1: Open Your Image in Photoshop

1. **Open Adobe Photoshop**: Open the Photoshop app on your device.

2. **Import Your Image:** Open **File > Open** and select the image you would want to work on. You can also simply drag and drop your image into Photoshop right from your **Explorer.**

3. **Duplicate the Background Layer**: To create a duplicate of your background layer, with which you can make edits non-destructively, right-click on the background layer and choose **Duplicate Layer** so that edits can be made without touching the original.

Step 2: Access the Crop Tool

1. **Select Crop Tool**: In the Tool Panel, select **Crop Tool**. The Crop tool icon resembles two overlapped right angles forming a square.

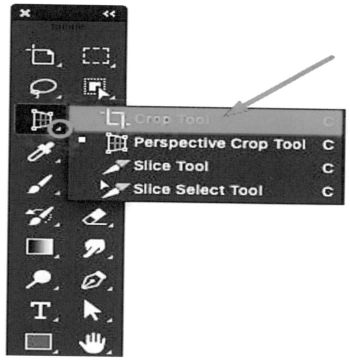

2. **Crop Box Adjustment:** Once you have clicked the Crop Tool, a crop box will frame around your image. The box contains handles at each corner and also on each side. With these handles, you could easily resize and sometimes even move the section of the crop.

Step 3: Adjust the Crop Box

1. **Set the Aspect Ratio:** You can specify an aspect ratio for the crop box on the options bar at the top. Click Unconstrained to crop in any ratio or one of the preset cropping ratios, such as 1:1, 4:5, and 16:9, with an intent to preserve specific dimensions.

    - **Custom Ratio:** Otherwise, you can specify your width and height specifications in the options bar to create a custom ratio that works best for you.

2. **Resize and Reposition**: To resize, click and drag any of the corner or side handles of the crop box. To move the entire box, click inside the box and drag it to the position.

Step 4: Straighten the Image (Correct Tilted Angles)

1. **Activate the Straighten Tool:** The Straighten Tool is incorporated into the Crop Tool in Adobe Photoshop 2025 to make adjustments in tilted horizons or slanted subjects.

2. **Choose the Straighten Option**: Click the **Straighten icon** in the options bar; it resembles a small ruler.

3. **Draw a Straightening Line**: Click and drag a line along that part of your picture that should be level, such as the horizon or a building edge. Photoshop automatically angles this line perfectly horizontally or perfectly vertically.

Step 5: Apply Content-Aware Crop (Optional)

1. **Activate Content-Aware Fill:** In case you want Photoshop to fill in the areas while cropping, check the option for Content-Aware in the option bar. It helps when the straightening of the image has left blank spaces near the edges.

2. **Auto Fill:** If Content-Aware is turned on, Photoshop will fill up the gaps by interpolation of surrounding pixels with the perfect extension of your image.

Note: Content-Aware Fill works best with blank spot backgrounds, or general landscapes since it uses Artificial Intelligence to guess what appropriate content could go in the blank area.

Step 6: Finalize Your Crop

1. **Review the Composition**: Take a general sense of framing and alignment. Adjust the crop box, when needed, to keep the attention of the picture on the main subject.

2. **Apply the Crop**: Once satisfied with your crop and straighten the adjustment, press Enter, or if you're on a Mac, use the Return key. It will apply the crop and remove the parts that were cropped out, along with saving the image in its new dimensions.

3. **Undo if Necessary**: If you have to go back, simply go to the Edit menu and choose Undo Crop or hit **Ctrl+Z for Windows users or Cmd+Z for Mac users.**

Step 7: Additional Adjustments (Optional)

After having cropped and straightened, you may want to make further improvements to the image:

1. **Adjust Exposure and Contrast:** If after cropping your picture has turned out either too dark or way too light, go to **Image > Adjustments > Brightness/Contrast** to adjust it.

2. **Minor Corrections with Healing Brush**: Use the Spot Healing Brush Tool (F) and start checking for slight blemishes or unwanted objects that appear more prominent after cropping.

Step 8: Save Your Cropped and Straightened Image

1. **Save as Photoshop Format**: If you want to retain the layers for future editing, save your file as a PSD by going to the menu option **File > Save As**, then selecting Photoshop as the file type.

2. **Save as Standard Image Format**: If your image is ready to be shared or uploaded, save it as a JPEG or PNG. Go to **File > Export > Export As** and select your preferred format and resolution.

USING CONTENT-AWARE SCALING

Content-Aware Scaling is one of the cool tools within Adobe Photoshop that can be used to resize a picture without distorting key elements. It preserves important parts of the image, like people or objects, while filling areas around them.

Step 1: Open Your Image and Duplicate the Background Layer

1. **Open Your Image**: Select your image file under **File > Open**, and open it in Photoshop.

2. **Duplicate the Background Layer**: Once the image is open, duplicate the background layer. To do this, right-click on the **Background layer** in the Layers panel and select Duplicate Layer. This step is critical because it will preserve your original image and allow you to work non-destructively.

3. **Rename the Layer (Optional):** For organization, if you wish, you can rename the duplicated layer by double-clicking the layer name and typing a new name, such as "**Content-Aware Scaling**."

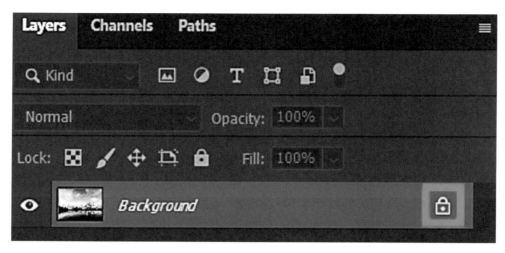

Step 2: Activate the Content-Aware Scaling

1. **Select Content-Aware Scaling:** With the moved layer active, click on the menu and select **Edit > Content-Aware Scale**. This activates the Content-Aware Scaling tool, evidenced by a bounding box around your image.

2. **Check the Options Bar:** When activated Content-Aware Scaling has options available along the top in the Options bar. If people are part of your image make sure to click **Protect Skin Tones**, which allows the scaling to retain the natural dimensions of the human form.

Step 3: Safeguard Key Features of the Image

1. **Safeguarding Elements with Alpha Channels**: To avoid scaling in those areas, you need to create an alpha channel. Select the protection area with any selecting tool like Quick Selection Tool and Lasso Tool.

2. **Save the Selection as an Alpha Channel:** Select your image, but make sure to have the selection active. Go to **Select > Save Selection**. Give the alpha channel a descriptive name - like "**Protected Area**" - and click **OK**. This lets Photoshop know which part of the image it should leave intact when resizing.

3. **Choose the Alpha Channel:** Find the Protect drop-down menu from the Options bar and select the alpha channel you just created. By setting this, you are letting Photoshop preserve the selection from distortion, especially when scaling.

Step 4: Begin Scaling with Content-Aware Scaling

1. **Scale the Image:** Drag any corner of the bounding box to scale the image. As it does, Photoshop begins to intelligently assess the content, stretching or compressing areas that aren't protected, thus leaving critical subjects intact.

2. **Adjust Proportionally**: To scale proportionally, hold the **Shift key** while dragging. This will maintain the aspect ratio of the original. To achieve even higher precision when transforming press the Width (W) and Height (H) options in the **Options bar** by typing in selected percentages or pixel values.

Step 5: Refined Scaling

1. **Inspect the Result:** After resizing, carefully check the image for unwanted distorting. Sometimes Content-Aware Scaling stretches minor background features, so you zoom in to check your image in all areas.

2. **Make Further Corrections**: If some parts of it need further corrections, do a slight Transform over that area of the image using **Edit > Free Transform.** By doing this you can adjust that part of your image which does not look natural after resizing it.

Step 6: Apply the Content-Aware Scaling

1. **Confirm the Changes:** When you are OK with the adjustments, press Enter or Return on Mac to commit the Content-Aware Scaling. You have now committed the change, but because you duplicate the background layer, you can always go back if you need to.

2. **Check the Image for Artifacts**: Check the final image to see if there are any visible artifacts or unexpected distortions. Sometimes, Content-Aware Scaling may have minor glitches, especially in complex patterns and textured backgrounds.

Step 7: Refining with Further Tools (Optional)

1. **Retouch with the Spot Healing and Clone Stamp Tools**: If some minor artifacts or weirdness are present, then go ahead and clean it up using the Spot Healing Brush or Clone Stamp Tool. This helps to merge areas flawlessly, which could have been disturbed around stretched edges.

2. **Layer Mask for Preciseness**: If there are areas where you would like to change, set a Layer Mask and mask on or off areas of your choosing. This is most helpful if parts of your image are slightly misshapen but are easy to mask in with a soft brush.

Step 8: Save Your Work

1. **Save the Project File:** It's always a good idea to save a working version of your image as a Photoshop (.PSD) file because that format retains layers and adjustments in case you revisit the project for further edits.

2. **Export the Final Image:** With the desired outcome, click **File > Export > Export As**, then save it in the format you need, like JPEG or PNG. Make sure that you set it according to your needs, like quality and resolution.

CHAPTER SIX

DRAWING AND PAINTING

HOW TO CREATE SHAPES

Step 1: Open Photoshop and Create a New Document

1. **Opening Photoshop:** Open **Adobe Photoshop 2025** on your computer.

2. **Creating a New Document**: Go to the **File** menu and select **New**.

3. **Document Settings:** Here, you can adjust the desired width, height, and resolution. Choose RGB for digital projects and CMYK for print.

4. **Select Background:** You will then select whether you want a white or transparent background depending on the needs of your project.

Create a new document with enough space to begin experimenting with various shapes and how you want them to interact in your image.

Step 2: Select the Shape Tool

1. **Identify the Shape Tool:** In the Tools panel, find the Shape tool. Its default icon is that of a rectangle, but holding down the icon will make other options appear.

2. **Reveal Shape Options:** Right-click or hold the Shape tool icon to see more options within this category:

    - **Rectangle Tool**: The customarily shaped rectangle.
    - **Ellipse Tool:** For circles and ovals.
    - **Polygon Tool:** Multi-Sided shapes.
    - **Line Tool:** Drawing straight lines.
    - **Custom Shape Tool:** To access and create custom shapes.

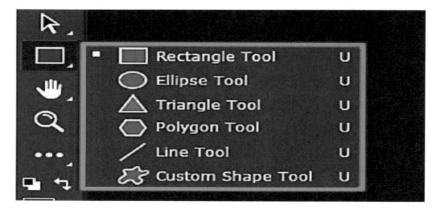

Step 3: Drawing Basic Shapes

1. **Choose a Shape Tool**: Let's start with the Rectangle Tool.
2. **Draw the Shape**:
    - Click and drag anywhere on the canvas to draw a rectangle.
    - To draw a square, click, and drag while holding the **Shift key** to constrain the shape.

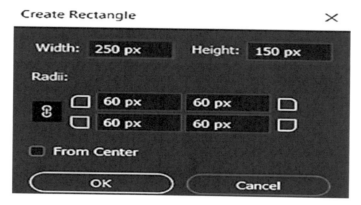

3. **Adjust Shape Settings:**
    - When you have drawn your shape, notice a new layer appears in the Layers panel. It can be manipulated independently.
    - The bounding box handles can now be used to scale the shape to whatever size you require.

These general steps also extend into the other shape tools. The Ellipse Tool will make circles if holding **Shift** and the Polygon Tool allows various numbers of sides.

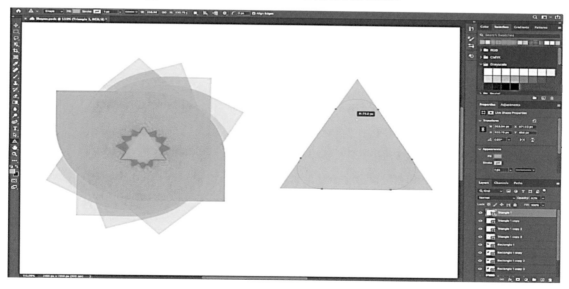

Step 4: Creating Shape Using the Options Bar

1. **Shape Properties:** Once a shape has been drawn the top options bar gives further ways to adjust.
   - **Stroke Color**: Add an outline to your shape, or edit an existing outline, by clicking to select a stroke color. You can change the width of the stroke to make it thicker or thinner.
   - **Shape Mode:** Select whether to create a new shape, add to the existing shape, subtract it, or intersect it with other overlapping shapes.
   - **Polygon Sides:** Using the options bar available when the Polygon Tool is selected, you can set the number of sides before creating the polygon. This is useful for creating triangles, which have 3 sides, or hexagons, which have 6 sides.
2. **Advanced Stroke Options**: Click the icon of the gear beside the stroke width option to select either solid, dashed, or dotted lines for creative borders.

Step 5: Working with the Custom Shape Tool

1. **Select the Custom Shape Tool**: Located in the Shape tool menu.
2. **Open Shape Library:**
   - The Shape Picker on the options bar opens an entire library of predefined shapes.
   - Photoshop 2025 has a huge collection of custom shapes, comprising arrows, stars, and other icons. At the bottom left corner of the Shape Picker, there is a gear icon to load more shapes or create your own.

3. **Draw the Custom Shape:**
   - Select any of the shapes in the Shape Picker and click and drag anywhere on the canvas.
   - To constrain proportions, hold **Shift**; to draw from the center outward, Alt.

Custom shapes have a great application in making quick designs, and icons, among other graphics that help to put across the beauty of your project.

Step 6: Editing Shape Properties

1. **Select Shape Layer**: In the Layers panel, click on a **Shape layer** so it's active.

2. **Edit Path Points:** The Direct Selection Tool is used by clicking the individual points along your shape's path. By doing this, one can edit it, hence achieving customized shapes.

3. **The Properties Panel:** Having any shape selected, one can open the **'Properties'** panel below; fill settings are presented with stroke and transformation. Shaping corner roundness for shapes like rectangles comes in handy when one wants to design items such as rounded buttons or frames.

Step 7: Combining Shapes Using the Path Operations

1. **Choose Multiple Shapes:** While holding **Shift**, click on each layer you want to merge in the Layers panel.
2. **Select a Path Operation**: Click to select a path operation icon from the options toolbar. You will see below four types:
   - **Add**: This tool will unify all the selected shapes as one shape.
   - **Subtract**: You can cut one shape out of the other.
   - **Intersect**: You can create only an overlapping part of the area.
   - **Exclude Overlapping Shapes**: You can only keep the parts that do not overlap and discard the rest.
3. **Apply and Finish:** These allow you to create complex forms and shapes without necessarily having to use a vector graphic editor.

The combination of shapes using path operations results in unlimited creative options.

Step 8: Converting Shapes into Smart Objects

1. **Right-Click on the Shape Layer**: Hit right-click on the shape layer that you want to turn into a Smart Object in the Layers panel.
2. **Select Convert to Smart Object**: You will activate non-destructive editing - using filters or transformations, for example without destroying the original shape.

Smart Objects are great for shapes that you want to continue to edit or add effects to because the object retains vector properties and can also be quickly reverted to its original form if changes need to be made.

Step 9: Rasterizing Shapes for Pixel-Based Editing

1. **Right-click the Shape Layer**: Right-clicking on the layer in the Layers panel will open an option to rasterize your shape and thereby enable you to edit your shape with pixel-based tools, like the Brush or Eraser tool.
2. **Choose Rasterize Layer:** This will convert the shape into a normal pixel layer that can be directly edited with pixel-based tools.

Keep in mind that rasterizing a shape converts it from vector to pixel and can lose quality when resized; therefore, it should be one of the last steps when you need precise edits.

Step 10: Saving Your Work

1. **Save as PSD**: If the project is in its ongoing stage, your file should be saved in PSD format because doing so will allow you to retain all layers and edits.
2. **Browse as PNG or JPEG**: For final use, such as web or print, export the shape design in PNG or JPEG format for easy sharing.

FILL AND STROKE SHAPES

Step 1: Creating a Shape

1. **Open Adobe Photoshop:** Open Photoshop and open a new project. Choose the dimensions and resolution according to your project requirements.

2. **Choose the Shape Tool:** The "**Shape Tool**" is in the left toolbar. By default, it's a rectangle icon. After clicking and dragging the icon down, additional shape choices appear in the drop-down menu - Rectangle, Ellipse, Polygon, Line, and Custom Shape Tools.

3. **Drawing Your Shape:** Under this menu, choose the shape you would want to trace out. Click and drag across your canvas, creating a new shape. You can adjust the size with the Shift key for maintaining proportions or, if you want free drawing, without the Shift key.

4. **Shapes Shape Properties**: In the "**Properties**" panel, which is on the right end of your screen, you will realize that there are several ways you can modify your shape. Two of the most important aspects are Fill and Stroke.

Step 2: Adding Fill to Your Shape

The property of Fill will define the inner color or texture of your shape. You can fill a shape with a solid color, gradient, or pattern.

1. **Open Fill Options**: Click on your shape layer to select it; either the right-hand side "**Properties**" panel or the top "**Options**" bar will open. The Fill section below will have the current fill color or style that your shape is using.

2. **Solid Color Fill:**
   - Click the Fill box; this will open a color picker where you can select a basic solid color from the spectrum or insert a specific hex code if you need an exact shade of color.
   - Once you have selected the color you want to use, click "**OK**" and it will fill your selected shape.

3. **Gradient Fill:**
   - Click the Fill box and then click "**Gradient**" under the fill type options.
   - You can open the Gradient Editor by clicking it to choose any of the preset gradients, or you make a custom one by editing color stops, opacity stops, and gradient direction.
   - The Properties panel provides the angle and scale of the gradient, which determines how the gradient will flow across the shape.

4. **Pattern Fill:**
   - You can enable the "**Pattern**" option in the Fill settings if you need to give it some texture.
   - Choose any from the Photoshop preloaded library or click on the "**Settings**" icon to load custom-created patterns.
   - Scale pattern for your design if needed, and blend options if necessary for special effects.

Step 3: Editing Stroke

The Stroke attribute will define how the outer line of the shape will look and where you will define the color, width, and style.

1. **Access Stroke Options:** In the "**Properties**" panel, next to where you had the Fill settings, you will have the Stroke box. Click it to access the options for Stroke.

2. **Set Stroke Color:**
   - Click the color box in the Stroke section; this will open the color picker.
   - Click on the color, type the hex code, or use the Photoshop eyedropper to click and select the color off the canvas.
   - Confirm the color by clicking "**OK**."

3. **Adjust Stroke Width**: This is below the color picker. You'll find the "**Width**" slider, where you can set the thickness of your stroke. Slide up or down through the slider to set the width desired, or you can type a specific value in pixels for precision.

4. **Stroke Style Options**:
   - Photoshop 2025 supports several stroke styles-solid, dashed, and dotted among others.
   - Click the "**More Options**" button (three dots) opening the advanced settings of Stroke, where you can edit dash and gap lengths or create a custom stroke pattern.

Step 4: Advanced Stroke Customization

Adobe Photoshop 2025 offers more options to cause strokes uniquely, such as aligning, blending, and layering strokes.

1. **Stroke Alignment:** You have options to put the stroke inside, outside, or centered on the path of the shape:
   - **Inside**: Completely within the boundary of the shape.
   - **Center**: The stroke straddles the edge of the shape.
   - **Outside**: The stroke is outside of the shape's edge.
   - **Align** according to your needs.

2. **Blending Options for Stroke**: Add blending options to give your stroke a more cohesive or striking look on your shape layer by doing the following steps:

   - Right-click the shape layer in the Layers panel, then select "**Blending Options**".
   - Click the "**Stroke**" option in the Layer Style window. Experiment with blending mode, opacity, and fill type to get a gradient or even a texture-like quality in the stroke.

3. **Layering Multiple Stroke**: You can stack multiple strokes within one single shape layer in Photoshop 2025 for complex designs.

   - You can click the "**+**" icon in the Stroke section of the Layer Style window to add multiple strokes.
   - Tweak every stroke individually to change the color, width, and blending effect that gives an object a layered or 3D appearance.

Step 5: Interactive Fill and Stroke in the Shape

After filling and stroking a shape, you may want to interactively change these properties as a part of your workflow.

1. **Choose the Direct Selection Tool**: In the toolbar above, click the "**Direct Selection Tool**" (white arrow icon) to enable this tool, allowing you to click on and edit an anchor point or path of the shape.

2. **Live Fill and Stroke Interaction**: Next, with your shape active, navigate back to the "**Properties**" panel, where you'll be able to make on-the-fly edits to the fill and stroke properties:

   - Try changing the fill color or gradient to observe what happens on the canvas.
   - Toggle stroke settings, like width or alignment; see immediate change

Step 6: Save and Export Shape

Now that your shape has been configured for fill and stroke just as you like, save it or export it for use in other projects or files.

1. **Save as a Custom Shape:** This shape, with all its fill and stroke settings, can be saved for later use in future projects by saving it as a custom shape:

   - Forward the selected shape layer to "**Edit**" > "**Define Custom Shape**."
   - Name and save it so that it can appear in the Photoshop "**Custom Shape Tool**" dropdown menu.

2. **Exporting the Shape:** You can export your stroked and filled shape by doing the following: Open "**File**" > "**Export**" > "**Export As.**"

- Select the required format, such as PNG, SVG, and JPEG. After choosing the format you want to export, now select the export settings, such as resolution and transparency.
- Click "**Export**" and save the file in your desired location.

DRAW A CUSTOM SHAPE

Step 1: Opening Adobe Photoshop and Creating a New Document

1. **Open Photoshop:** Open the Adobe Photoshop 2025 app. You can do this either from an application list or by shortcut.

2. **Create a New Document**: Under "**File**" click "**New**" or Ctrl + N for Windows/Cmd + N for Mac. Choose the dimensions, resolution, and color mode that best fit the project you are working on:

   - **Dimensions**: Make it 1000 pixels by 1000 pixels if designing a web graphic.
   - **Resolution**: Pick 300 pixels per inch for printing, or 72 pixels per inch if it will be used online.
   - **Color Mode**: Select RGB if your graphics will be viewed on screen, or select CMYK if they are to print. Click "**Create**" to display your new canvas.

Step 2: Select the Custom Shape Tool

1. **Open the Shape Tool:** This should be available in the left toolbar and should most often be defaulted to the Rectangle Tool.

2. **Choose the Custom Shape Tool**: Then click and hold on to the Rectangle Tool icon until you see your additional shape options come up, then click on "**Custom Shape Tool**".

3. **Adjust Settings**: You'll notice at the top there is an options bar that indicates what can be customized for the Custom Shape Tool. You can adjust:

   - **Fill**: With the color or gradient, you choose.
   - **Stroke**: Outline color, width, and style - solid, dashed, dotted.
   - **Path Options**: Choose whether you want your path to be a shape, a path, or pixels.

Step 3: Using a Predefined Shape or Making Your Own

1. **Open Shape Presets**: Once the Custom Shape Tool is engaged, a shape chooser icon appears on the options bar at the top.

2. **Browse Shapes**: Adobe Photoshop 2025 has a set of in-built shapes running the gamut from arrows to animals, speech bubbles, and symbols. You can browse through categories for what is provided.

3. **Download More Shapes**: Photoshop may let you download more shapes directly from the Creative Cloud with its updated version. You can also click on the gear icon inside the shape selector and select "**Get More Shapes**" to add more to your library.

4. **Create a Custom Shape**: You can also design a shape from scratch using the Pen Tool and save it as a custom shape.

Step 4: Draw Your Shape

1. **Position Your Cursor**: Move your cursor to the area of the canvas where you want to start drawing.

2. **Click and Drag**: Click and drag to draw the shape. Holding the **Shift key** down will constrain proportions, making squares or circles from rectangles and ellipses.

3. **Resize and Rotate (Optional):** After having drawn the shape, make use of the transform controls to resize, rotate, or reposition the shape as needed. To do this, use Ctrl + T for Free Transform mode on Windows, or Cmd + T on Mac, and perform your adjustment.

Step 5: Refine Shape with Properties Panel

1. **Open Properties Panel:** Open up the Properties panel by first selecting your shape layer and then heading to "**Window**" > "**Properties**".

2. **Edit Shape Properties:** In this panel, you can define a shape by first entering your width and height, then proceed with adjusting the fill and stroke color along with the weight of your shape.

3. **Try Stroke Styles:** One can utilize the Stroke dropdown menu to try experimenting with various line styles, inclusive of solid lines, dashes, and dotted outlines for added effect.

Step 6: Creating Your Custom Shape (Optional)

1. **Use the Pen Tool**: Click on and select the Pen Tool from the toolbar. In the top bar, it should be set to "**Shape**" mode.

2. **Draw Your Shape:** Just click to add anchor points and outline the shape. If you drag while clicking it will create curves instead of straight lines.

3. **Complete the Shape**: Connect the path back to the start to complete the shape.

4. **Save as a Custom Shape:** Right-click on your new shape layer and select "**Define Custom Shape.**" Name it in the dialog box that opens. Your shape will now be saved to the shape presets for later use in future projects.

Step 7: Stylize Your Shape

1. **Apply Layer Styles**: Once your shape layer is selected, go to "**Layer**" > "**Layer Style**" and open the menu for Drop Shadow, Bevel & Emboss, Gradient Overlay, and so on.

2. **Try Effects:** Try adding various effects that would give depth or texture to your shape. For example, you can give your shape a Drop Shadow to pick it off of a page more, while a Gradient Overlay would add color variation.

3. **Adjust Opacity and Blend Modes**: Add partial transparency to your shape with the use of the Opacity slider in the Layers panel. You may also try checking Multiply or Screen blend modes to see how your shape interacts with other elements on the canvas.

Step 8: Distort Shape Using Warp and Transform

1. **Use Warp Mode:** Click on "**Edit**" > "**Transform**" > "**Warp**" and use control points to reshape the custom shape.

2. **Play with Warp Options:** Warping options in Photoshop 2025 are so advanced; hence, they will let you stretch, twist, and distort the shape by dragging points.

Step 9: Duplicate and Arrange Shapes

1. **Duplicate Shape**: First select the shape layer and use Ctrl + J for Windows or Cmd + J for Mac. This will be helpful if you need more than one of these particular shapes.

2. **Align Copies**: Drag duplicates across the canvas, moving and placing them. Use alignment tools in the Options bar to keep everything aligned and neat.

3. **Merging Shapes**: To create complex compositions, use the Shape Builder Tool or select **Layer > Combine Shapes**. Select to add, subtract, intersect, and exclude to create special compositions.

Step 10: Save and Export Your Work

1. **Save Your Photoshop Document**: Save your document as a PSD through "**File**" > "**Save As**" to retain all layers and editability.

2. **Export for Web or Print**: Finally, to create the final output, go to "**File**" > "**Export**" > "**Export As.**" Choose the format according to your needs: JPEG, PNG, SVG, etc. Now, modify some export settings such as quality, resolution, and color space as per your requirements for web or print purposes.

3. **Save Shape for Future Use**: In case you want to use your design in some other project, highlight the shape layer and right-click to save it as a custom shape or add it to a shape library.

SELECTING CURSOR PREFERENCES

Step 1: Open Adobe Photoshop

Start by launching Adobe Photoshop 2025. If you have this application on your desktop or in your taskbar, highlight the icon and click.

If not, browse in your applications folder and open the application from there. Make sure you have no unsaved opened projects to avoid any prompts getting in the way as you go through the preferences.

Step 2: Open the Preferences Menu

Click the **Preferences** menu. The Preferences menu contains all options for customizing various features in the application. How to locate it on various operating systems:

- **For Windows Users**: Click the **Edit** menu at the top, scroll down, and click **Preferences > Cursors**.

- **For Mac Users**: Tap the Photoshop menu on the top left corner of the screen, then select **Preferences**, then **Cursors**.

This will open the main Preferences window, which contains a lot of settings for various tools and workflows in Photoshop.

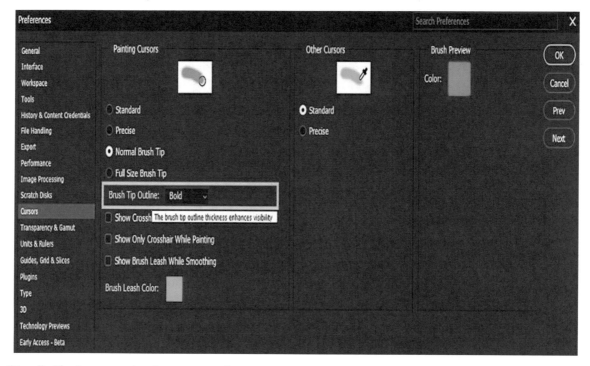

Step 3: Navigate to the Cursors Section

In the Preferences window, on the left-hand side, various categories can be observed. Click Cursors to open settings to customize cursors. Cursor settings in Photoshop can be modified to change how the cursor would appear for different functions, such as painting, selecting items, moving them, etc., on the canvas. You can set three main types of cursors here, namely: Painting Cursors, Other Cursors, and Brush Tip Options.

Step 4: Adjust the Painting Cursor Settings

The Painting cursor preference determines the display of the cursor when the painting tools such as the Brush, Pencil, and Eraser, among others, are selected.

Here are the options that you will find:

- **Standard**
  The Standard cursor depicts the tool icon as the cursor. For example, if you happen to be using the Brush tool, it shows a small icon of a brush as the cursor. This is helpful when one is still a beginner and wants a clear visual reminder of what tool they have selected.
- **Precise**
  The Precise cursor changes the icon to a crosshair giving you an exact point of reference where the action will take place. This is useful when doing close detailed work in places where you need to be most precise with your brush strokes or selections.
- **Normal Brush Tip**
  The cursor is a grayed-out outline of the shape of the brush, sized to your chosen size of the brush. This is a good medium for showing the brush shape and its size clearly on the canvas.
- **Full-Size Brush Tip**
  The Full-Size Brush Tip option will show the outline of the brush full size, considering feathering or soft edges.
  - This setting is really good for an artist who needs to see the entire effect of their stroke, especially when using softer brushes with larger feathered edges.
  - Click the radio button beside one of the three Painting Cursor choices to select your preference. Immediately Photoshop will set your preference that you can instantly try out by selecting a painting tool on your canvas.

Step 5: Adjusting the Other Cursor Preferences

The Other Cursors setting sets the behavior of your cursor when you are using any tool that is not a painting tool, such as selection tools, the Pen tool, and shape tools.

Step 6: Refining the Brush Tip Options

Even more refinement to the settings can be done within Photoshop with brush tip options that can allow the look of your cursor in using brush-like tools to be tailored even more closely.

Here are the Brush Tip Options that you can apply:

- **Show Crosshair in Brush Tip**
  With the Show Crosshair in the Brush Tip option selected, you pop up a small crosshair dead center of the brush tip. Many times, this is quite useful as one wants to see visually the size of the brush but also have an exact point of reference for the brush's center. This

is especially useful when applying effects in tight areas because now you can align the center of the brush more precisely.

- **Show Only Crosshair While Painting**
    - The Show Only Crosshair While Painting option will toggle the brush tip to only show the crosshair while you're actively painting. This setting reduces distraction and allows for a greater focus on making more precise movements, particularly when working on small details.
    - To activate any of these, check the box beside your preference by clicking it. Both of these features are optional and may be left unchecked if you desire a more minimalistic view.

Step 7: Apply and Test Your Settings

- Once you have the cursor settings to your liking, click OK to save and apply the changes. Immediately, Photoshop will refresh your cursor preferences and allow you to test the new settings by selecting a few different tools to see how the cursor behaves with each.
- If you don't like your changes or if you want to play around with other cursor settings, you're free to return to the Preferences menu anytime.

Step 8: Additional Tips for Cursor Settings

- **Switch Between Precise and Standard Cursor:** If you do a lot of work with both precise and standard cursors, then use the Caps Lock shortcut. When you press Caps Lock, it toggles the mode on or off; so, you can switch between them in no time.
- **Think About Monitor Size:** When working on a large monitor, selecting a full-size brush tip can make it easier to spot a cursor, while smaller monitors are better off with a smaller brush tip or the precise cursor setting.
- **Use Crosshairs for Fine Detail:** When working on tasks where you want to work in some detail, like when masking or retouching, the facilitation of working with much more accuracy will come from enabling crosshairs, due to the central reference point it gives, which is very helpful when trying to work on fine details or small areas.

Step 9: Saving Your Cursor Options

- After rigorously testing your preferences with the cursor, you will know what to do to have those settings optimized for your workflow. If you feel that some settings are not performing as well as you had perceived, go back into **Preferences > Cursors** and make the changes.
- A properly set cursor can save a lot of time and increase productivity; therefore, take all the necessary time to find a configuration that works most effectively with your editing style and project needs.

IMPORT BRUSHES AND BRUSH PACKS

Step 1: Locating and Downloading Brush Packs

Before importing brushes into Photoshop, you need to locate and download a brush pack.

Adobe Photoshop can support a variety of different brush file types, namely: ABBR, or Adobe Brush, files. You can find brush packs from Adobe's official resources and Adobe Creative Cloud Libraries but also from independent creators and art platforms and design websites like DeviantArt, Behance, and Gumroad.

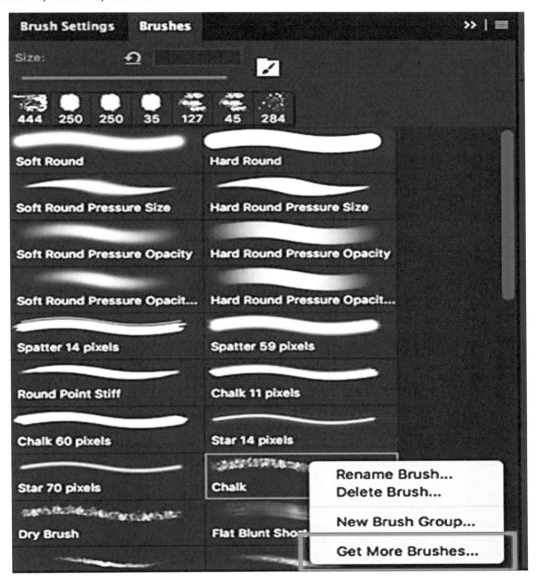

- **Adobe Creative Cloud Library**: Having Adobe's Creative Cloud subscription will grant you access to a vast collection of free and paid brushes. You can search for them by opening the Libraries panel inside Photoshop, then Discover Brushes.
- **Third-party Websites**: Several design websites offer amazing and unique brushes. Make sure that the files downloaded are compatible **.ABR format** with Photoshop.

Step 2: Save Brushes to an Organized Location

Once the files of the brushes have been downloaded, save them in a folder created for that purpose. In this way, it will be easy to access the file. This helps you to be organized and not frustrated-especially when you need to switch between different brush packs, or when you need to reinstall your brushes at any given point in time.

1. **Create a New Folder**: Go to a location on your computer, such as Documents or a folder you may have or will create for Photoshop resources, and create a new folder. Name it "**Photoshop Brushes**" or whatever you like.

2. **House Your Brushes**: You will take your downloaded **.ABR files** and either move them or save them into this folder. Keeping all your brushes in one place not only keeps them organized but also makes it easier to find when you need them.

Step 3: Accessing Photoshop and Open the Brushes Panel

After having prepared your brush files, open Adobe Photoshop and prepare to import the new brushes.

1. **Open Photoshop**: Open Photoshop 2025 as you would normally do.

2. **Open Brushes Panel**: In the top toolbar, click on the **Window menu,** then select **Brushes**. This will open the Brushes panel, showing you the default list of available brushes in Photoshop.

3. **Brush Preset Manager:** You can also open the Brush Preset Manager to manage and edit your collection of brushes. The Brushes panel, though, has more options for editing and importing directly.

Step 4: Importing Brushes

There are various ways you can import your brushes into Photoshop 2025. You could be adding just one .ABR file or a pack of brushes. Do whichever is easier for you.

Method 1: Drag and Drop

Simple and works great if you're in a hurry to import something.

1. **Open Folder:** Open the folder in which your **.ABR brush file** is located.

2. **Drag the File:** Click and drag the **.ABR file** into the open workspace area of Photoshop. Automatically, it will detect the file type and load the brushes into your Brushes panel.

3. **Locate Your Brushes**: Once the import is complete, the new brushes will be added to the Brushes panel, often as a new folder or group with the name of the brush pack.

Method 2: Import through the Brushes Panel

If you're more into the traditional method, you can import them directly from the Brushes panel.

1. **Go to Brushes Panel Menu**: Click on the three-line menu icon at the top right of the Brushes panel to open the menu options available in this panel.

2. **Select Import Brushes**: Click on **Import Brushes** from the pull-down menu.

3. **On the Left, Go to Your Brush Folder:** In the file dialog that opens, navigate to your designated brush folder, and select the .ABR file you want to import and click Open.

4. **Confirm Import:** The brushes will load into Photoshop, and they should now be available in the Brushes panel.

Method 3: Using Adobe Creative Cloud Library

If you downloaded your brushes through Adobe's Creative Cloud Libraries, then they are accessible directly within Photoshop.

1. **Open the Libraries Panel**: Go to **Window > Libraries** to open your Adobe Libraries.

2. **Locate Your Brushes**: Once you download the pack of brushes, it should appear in your Libraries. You can drag them into the Brushes panel or you can double-click on them to load the brushes.

Step 5: Organizing Imported Brushes

Once you have imported your brushes, you can then organize your brushes inside the Brushes panel for ease of access.

1. **Create Group for Brushes**: Go to the Brushes panel, and click the bottom icon of Folder creation to create a new group. You can name this folder with any name about the brush type, such as "**Watercolor Brushes**" or "**Sketching Brushes.**"

2. **Move the Brushes into the Group**: Now, select the imported brushes and drag these into the newly created folder to organize them.

3. **Edit Brush Settings**: Right-clicking on each of the brushes allows for renaming, and changing their size and spacing amongst other settings, which may be helpful for you to personalize the brushes for your use.

Step 6: Testing and Adjusting Brushes

Once you have imported your brushes, it will be quite helpful if you try them for you to see if they meet your needs.

1. **Choose a Brush**: Click to select any of the brushes in the Brushes panel.

2. **Adjust Brush Settings**: The attributes of shape dynamics, scattering, texture, and dual brush are fine-tuned using the Brush Settings panel via Window · Brush Settings. Advanced features on the Brush Settings panel in Photoshop 2025 enable fine settings.

3. **Test New Document:** Create a new open document and play with your new set of brushes to be acquainted with the behavior of each brush. This is made for one to identify which brushes will be more suitable for which projects.

Step 7: Organizing and Deleting Brushes

When one feels some brushes are of no good use, it's very easy to delete or even reset your library of brushes.

1. **Right-click to Delete:** On the Brushes panel, right-click a brush that you want to eliminate and choose **Delete Brush**.

2. **Reset Brushes:** To delete all your created brushes and return to Photoshop's default set of brushes, in the menu for the Brushes panel choose Reset Brushes and confirm your selection.

Step 8: Save Your Customized Brush Set

To preserve your customized brush setup, save it as a special brush set.

1. **Create a New Set**: To do so, go to the Brushes panel menu and select **Export Selected Brushes**. This will save your custom brushes as an **.ABR file.**

2. **Save Location**: After selecting a location in which you would like this new **.ABR file** to be saved, you'll always be able to reload your customized brush set in any case of reinstating Photoshop or using your brushes with another machine.

CREATE A BRUSH TIP FROM AN IMAGE

Step 1: Select the Image

1. **Choose an Image**: First, select an image containing any texture, shape, or pattern that would suit a brush tip.

   Everything from cloud patterns to foliage, and fabric textures, right down to a hand-drawn sketch will do just fine. Just remember that high-contrast images with definite edges will work best when generating brushes.

2. **Open Image in Photoshop:** First, open Adobe Photoshop and then load the image file that you will use for your brush. Go to **File > Open** and select your image.

Step 2: Prepare the Image

1. **Adjust Contrast:** Go to **Image > Adjustments > Levels** or **Image > Adjustments > Brightness/Contrast**. Any of these sliders can be moved to increase the contrast between the foreground (what you want as your brush tip) and the background. This will start to create a better isolation of the texture or shape you want in your brush.

2. **Convert to Grayscales:** While not necessary, making an image grayscale makes focusing on shape and texture much easier. Go to **Image > Mode > Grayscale**, choosing Discard when prompted. Because brushes in Photoshop do not capture color, this will help make sure the final brush appearance will be clearer.

3. **Define Shape and Edges:** Choose your favorite selecting tool (Lasso Tool or Quick Selection Tool) to draw around the selections in the picture that you want to include in the brush. Go to **Edit > Copy,** and **Edit > Paste** on a new layer with your selection.

Step 3: Refine and Clean Up the Shape

1. **Use Layer Masking:** When you want to refine the shape, click the Layer Mask icon at the bottom of the Layers panel. With this done, use a black brush to mask parts of the image or a white one to reveal the parts of the image and refine the edges of your brush to fine-tune the areas more aptly.

2. **Remove Backgrounds and Clean Edges**: The Eraser Tool or Select and Mask can be utilized in ridding the image of unwanted areas and smoothing out edges so that the brush tip looks well-defined and clean.

3. **Blur or Sharpen as Required**: Under Filter, choose either **Blur** or **Sharpen** to adjust the softness or definition of the texture. Light blurring tends to create soft brush tips while sharpening enhances the fine details.

Step 4: Define the Brush Tip

1. **Select the Shape**: Once you are satisfied with your shape, select it by holding down Ctrl (Cmd on Mac) + Clicking on the layer thumbnail. This will select all of the shapes that you have created.

2. **Define the Brush:** Go to **Edit > Define Brush Preset**. In the open dialog box, name your new brush. For example, **"Leaf Texture"** or **"Rough Edge"**. Click OK to save the brush. Now, a custom brush tip has been created and is present in the Brushes Panel.

Step 5: Adjust the Brush Settings

1. **Open the Brush Setting Panel**: Open **Window > Brush Settings** to put in the settings that you can apply to your brush. You can edit, among others, spacing, shape dynamics, scattering, and texture here.

2. **Modify Shape Dynamics**: Under Shape Dynamics, you can adjust the size jitter, angle jitter, and other parameters to add random variation in each click of the brush. This will be useful if you are creating a natural organic appearance, it may be foliage or clouds.

3. **Use Scattering:** Checkmark Scattering to scatter multiple instances of the brush tip for each stroke. You move the Count and Count Jitter sliders to specify the density of the scatter effect.

4. **Texture Settings**: By clicking the Texture, you add another texture to your brush tip. You can choose the defaults or import any of your own to give the brush an added texture.

5. **Transfer Settings:** The Transfer option allows you to adjust each stroke of the brush's opacity and flow so that, with a little pressure sensitivity if you are using a drawing tablet, the softness or heaviness will be reflected in the brushstrokes.

Step 6: Saving the Custom Brush

1. **Create a New Brush Group**: If you're going to be designing more than one custom brush, you can create a new group for them. Through the Brushes panel open, click on the **Brush Group Folder Icon**, name it, and drag this custom brush into that group for organization.

2. **Create Your Brush Preset**: Once you have reached your perfect setting, you can save a preset of this brush. You can click the **Create New Brush icon** at the top in the Brush Setting Panel, check off all of the settings that you have adjusted, title your brush, and click **OK** to save.

Step 7: Test Your Brush

1. **Create a New Document:** To create a new document, go to **File > New**. Here, you set your document dimensions and resolution.

2. **Play with Your Brush:** Go ahead and choose your new brush via the Brushes Panel to start painting on the canvas. Experiment with different settings, pressures, and strokes to get familiar with how it will act.

3. **Refine if Needed:** Every time you spot an anomaly, you may want to return to the **'Brush Settings'** panel and change any one of these settings: If, for instance, the feel of the brush is too spaced out or close together, adjust the **'Spacing'** setting. Do this until it meets your artistic needs.

Step 8: Save the Brush as Part of a Set

1. **Save a Brush Set**: Save a brush set if you are going to make more custom brushes or want to create a collection of custom brushes. Within the Brushes Panel click the **Preset Manager** and select all the brushes in the set you want to save.

2. **Export Your Brush Set:** While having the brushes selected, click Save Set and name your set. Save it in a location where you can easily access it for future projects or to share it with others.

CLEAR BRUSH OPTIONS

Step 1: Open Adobe Photoshop 2025 and Access Brush Settings

Before proceeding to begin working with adjusting the brush settings, make sure that Adobe Photoshop 2025 is open and a project or canvas ready. First of all, you need to access the settings of the Brush via the panel, which will show every setting and customization you are going to use with your brushes. Here's how you do it:

1. **Choose the Brush Tool**: You can access settings after selecting the Brush Tool first by pressing **B** on your keyboard or via the Tools panel where the Brush Tool is located.

2. **Open Brush Settings:** In the top menu bar, click the **Window menu** and select **Brush Settings** from the drop-down list that opens. It opens the Brush Settings panel to show all available options for brushes.

Step 2: Resetting Brush Attributes in the Brush Settings Panel

Within the Brush Settings panel, you can refine several attributes: Shape Dynamics, Scattering, Texture, Dual Brush, and many others. If you want to clean up any adjustments you have made, you can either reset each attribute separately or apply a complete reset.

1. **Individual Reset:** Deactivate an attribute by unchecking its check box in the Brush Preset Picker or Brush Settings panel. If you have Scattering and you want it off, uncheck the checkbox for no scattering effects from your brush.

2. **Full Reset:** If you have done a lot of customization in various attributes, you might want to reset them all to their default settings. Click the **Brush Presets panel**; often this is located beside the Brush Settings panel. Once you have opened the Brush Presets panel, click the gear icon at the top right of the Brush Presets panel. A drop-down menu will appear in which you'll select Reset Brushes.

Note: This will automatically reset every setting related to the brush back to its default state; therefore, if you have any custom brushes saved, it's a good idea to save them before doing this.

Step 3: Clear Brush Styles in the Brush Panel

The Brush panel houses your pre-made brush styles. These can be edited or imported from outside sources. If you want to clear a single style or even reset the entire library for your brush, here's how:

1. **Clear Some Brushes:** For this, first activate the menu by clicking **Window > Brushes**. Then, right-click a specific brush variant and further click on **Delete Brush**.

2. **Reset Brush Library**: To return to the default brush library settings, click on the icon at the top right of the Brushes panel and click on Reset Brushes. This will overwrite any imported or modified brushes with the default Photoshop set.

If you would like to save your customized brushes for later, it's a good idea to save them as a brush set by clicking on the gear icon and choosing "**Export Selected Brushes**."

Step 4: Using Brush Tip Shape to Clear Custom Brush Settings

Photoshop allows you to modify the brush tip shape in several ways to create custom effects related to each brush. To undo or clear any specific brush tip shape modification:

1. **Choose Brush Tip Shape:** Under the Brush menu option, available on the left-hand side of the Brush Settings panel, select the **'Brush Tip Shape'** setting.

2. **Adjust to Default Shape**: Set to default shape with the Diameter and Hardness sliders or choose one of the default circular options within the tip shape gallery.

3. **Reset Angle and Roundness**: If you have adjusted the angle or roundness, click to restore to 100% to clear any applied tilt effect.

Step 5: Reset Brush Dynamics Settings

The Brush Dynamics settings change how your brush responds to specific conditions, like pressure or angle.

To begin anew, take away any dynamics settings that are already applied:

1. **Open Dynamics Options:** Open the Shape Dynamics or one of the other dynamics menu options, such as Transfer or Color Dynamics from the Brush Settings window.

2. **Turn Off All Dynamics Settings**: Deselect the checkbox next to every dynamic setting. For example, when Shape Dynamics is turned on, its checkbox clears to straighten and even out size and angle based on pressure sensitivity.

Note: If you are using a tablet, disabling dynamics will affect how your brush responds to pen pressure.

Step 6: Reset Brush Texture and Dual Brush

Photoshop's texture and dual brush settings establish unique textures or combinations for detailed effects.

You can reset these settings to provide a cleaner brush:

1. **Clear Texture:** Enter the Settings from the Texture menu option. Disable the check mark to eliminate an applied texture effect.

2. **Remove Dual Brush:** Similarly, check Dual Brush then uncheck to turn it off.

By Deselecting these, it will clear the option and let your brush use only its major shape and dynamics without any effects.

Step 7: Save a Custom Reset Brush as Default

After unchecking all the customizations, save the brush to have a custom default for later use. These will give you a fresh or blank brush to start with every time.

1. **Open the Brush Presets Panel**: Once everything is reset, open the Brush Preset panel.

2. **Save Brush as New Preset:** This is done by clicking the bottom of the Brush Presets panel and naming the brush, "**Default Reset Brush.**"

3. **Use as Default:** Making this the default opening brush in Photoshop is as simple as selecting it from the Brush Presets panel.

ADD DYNAMIC ELEMENTS TO BRUSHES

Adobe Photoshop 2025 offers new and exciting features, one of which is the ability for brushes to be highly flexible and dynamic. The tool allows one to add responsive changes within the brush strokes when certain settings such as pressure, tilt, scatter, texture, and many more come into play. It is a feature that is priceless for a wide range of artists, designers, and people who generally want to give their creations some level of organic spontaneity.

Step 1: Open the Brush Settings Panel

1. Open Adobe Photoshop 2025 and create/open a document.

2. Open the menu by heading to **Window > Brush Settings**. Here, you will manage all aspects of your brush, everything from size to new dynamic elements.

3. Click to choose a brush from the Brush Presets or to create a new one. Although you can always change this later, naturally you want to select a brush that best fits the style you're trying to achieve. A soft round will give a very different effect than a textured or rough one, for example.

Step 2: Enable Shape Dynamics

Shape dynamics control the size, angle, and roundness of the brush while you paint. You can link the settings to the pressure, tilt, or any of the other input devices.

1. Select the **Shape Dynamics check box** in the Brush Settings panel.

2. **Specify the following options:**

   - **Size Jitter:** This allows the size of every stroke to vary. Place this to the Pen Pressure if you're on a tablet to adjust the size of your brush depending on how hard you press.
   - **Angle Jitter**: Vary the angle of the brush tip to have a more organic feel to it. You can set it to Initial Direction so the angle adjusts based on the direction you're moving the brush.
   - **Roundness Jitter**: Controls the roundness or squishiness of the brush. This helps in having a natural variation similar to when brush fibers would spread across a canvas.

This can be used to obtain variation within a stroke, to achieve effects that are akin to pencil sketches or even charcoal.

Step 3: Add Scattering

Scattering allows the brush tip to spread across the canvas, creating an effect like splattering paint or applying scattered textures.

1. In the Brush Settings panel, check **Scattering**.

2. Drag the Scatter slider to specify the amount of scatter. The higher the value, the farther apart the brush marks spread out.

3. Set **Count Jitter** to determine how many brush marks appear for each stroke. With a high Count and low scattering, you get a tight and clustered appearance; with a low Count and high scattering, you can achieve the effect of spray paint.

This is ideal for painting grass, stars, leaves of all descriptions, or anything else that you want to appear random. Adding randomness increases the realism of this subject.

Step 4: Adjust Texture Dynamics

Textured brushes can simulate the surface you are working on by applying texture to each stroke, like canvas or watercolor paper.

1. In the Brush Settings panel turn on the Texture option.

2. Select a default pattern from the Pattern Picker or load your own.

3. You can also use the Scale and Depth settings to adjust how prominent the texture is on your stroke.

4. Enable **Texture Dynamics** to randomize the pattern across each stroke. You can further refine this with Depth Jitter and Contrast.

5. The Blend Mode for a texture will set the way it interacts with the color of the brush.

Textures go along great with natural media emulation to help you achieve realistic paint effects or rugged surfaces.

Step 5: Experiment with Dual Brush Dynamics

Dual Brush allows the ability to combine two brushes to achieve an interesting effect. It can create complex textures or other shapes within each stroke.

1. Check **Dual Brush** in the Brush Settings panel.

2. Open **Brush Picker** and select a secondary brush.

3. Adjust Size, Spacing, Scatter, and Count to see how the dual brush interacts with the main brush. You can achieve everything from soft, diffused patterns to sharp and detailed work.

4. Play with various combinations to achieve the effect you need. For example, take a textured brush and add a round brush for an ink bleed paper effect.

Dual brushes are especially useful for those effects that require an 'extended' or multi-layer look, such as stippling or texturing leaves.

Step 6: Color Dynamics for Vibrant, Many-Colored Strokes

Color Dynamics enable your brush to change color while you paint, thereby providing vibrant, multi-colored effects.

1. In the Brush Settings panel, make sure the Color Dynamics check box is enabled.

2. **Hue Jitter**: Introduces color variation with each stroke of the tool. The higher the value, the more variation in color change, and vice versa.

3. **Saturation Jitter**: The use of saturation to provide more depth and colorfulness in strokes.

4. **Brightness Jitter**: Provides variance in lightness/darkness levels. This is useful when painting natural features like foliage or water, where there can be subtle color variations that occur for something to appear natural.

5. Allow **Purity** to enable purity to control the saturation or brightness of your colors.

Color dynamics are nice for fantasy artwork, or any scene for that matter, in which colors should feel more organic and alive.

Step 7: Transfer Controls for Responsive Brushstrokes

Transfer controls allow your brush opacity or flow to vary depending on pressure or tilt, among other things to add subtlety to your strokes.

1. Under the **Brush Settings panel**, beneath **Transfer**.

2. Use the **Opacity Jitter** to specify how transparent or opaque each stroke may be, considering the amount of pressure applied.

3. Use **Flow Jitter** to introduce variation in color flow across strokes. The result will usually blend or soften.

4. If you are dealing with a tablet, enable Control for pen pressure to make opacity and flow react to your pressure.

These settings come into play particularly when dealing with airbrush effects, watercolor emulation, or any technique that relies on opacity control.

Step 8: Save and Export Your Customized Brush

When your dynamic settings are just right, save your brush for later use:

1. Click the menu for Brush Settings (three little lines icon) at the top right of the Brush Settings panel.

2. Choose **New Brush Preset** and name your new brush.

3. The brush will be saved now in the **'Brush Preset'** panel and will be ready for use whenever you need it.

CHAPTER SEVEN

VIDEO AND ANIMATION

HOW TO EDIT VIDEOS IN PHOTOSHOP

Step 1: Importing Your Video into Photoshop

1. **Open Photoshop:** Open Photoshop 2025 from either the desktop or applications folder.

2. **Import the Video File:** Go to **File > Open** and navigate to the video file that you wish to edit. Photoshop supports a wide variety of formats for opening videos, which include MP4 and MOV.

3. **Playing the Timeline**: When you open your video in Photoshop, it automatically opens as a layer in the Layers Panel. To activate and start working with the timeline of your video, you need to open the timeline panel at the bottom of your screen by selecting Window>Timeline. The Create Video Timeline button will change your video layer into a timeline format.

Step 2: Working with the Timeline Interface

Most of your video editing is to be done on the Timeline panel. Familiarizing yourself with some of its more important features will help to smooth out your workflow:

1. **Playhead**: The red line shows where in the video you currently are. Drag it along the timeline to show you a preview of different frames.

2. **Layers in Timeline:** Similar to layers in the Layers panel, each new video clip, image, or text will appear as a separate layer within the timeline.

3. **Zoom Slider**: This allows you to zoom the timeline in and out; this is very useful for making finer edits.

4. **Layer Trimming:** This involves altering the length of a clip by dragging the edges of the video layer in the timeline.

5. **Playback Controls**: Use the play, pause, and stop buttons to review your edits.

Step 3: Basic Edits – Trimming, Splitting and Rearranging Clips

With your timeline now set up, you can trim, split, and rearrange clips in basic edits.

1. **Trim Video**: Click the video layer in the timeline to begin the cut either from the beginning or from the end of the video. Then, drag the beginning or end of the layer toward your preferred position.

You can split clips by moving the playhead to any point at which you wish to cut, then right-clicking and selecting **Split at Playhead**.

2. **Reordering Clips**: If you happen to have several video files or layers open, you can reorder these easily using drag and drop along the timeline.

3. **Add Additional Clips:** To add additional video clips, images, or text go to **Layer > Video Layers > New Video Layer from File**.

Step 4: Adding Image Adjustments to Videos

Probably one of the most useful features of Photoshop for video editing is that you have a huge range of image adjustments you can make and apply to every frame in your video.

1. **Choose the Video Layer:** The first thing you want to do is select the video layer, and you'll click on the video layer on the layers panel.

2. **Add an Adjustment Layer:** To add an adjustment layer, click on **Layer > New Adjustment Layer**; from here, you can choose Brightness/Contrast, Levels, Color Balance, and many other choices that you want to give your video a different appearance.

3. **Customize Adjustments**: Change the setting of the adjustment layer to suit your desired look. The adjustment layers, by default, affect all frames of the video located below it.

4. **Blending Modes and Opacity**: For special effects, experiment with blending modes and opacity for your Adjustment Layers.

Step 5: Add Text Overlay

In Photoshop, you can add text overlays that would be useful for adding several things like captions and titles to your video in the form of text.

1. **Select the Type Tool:** The Type Tool can be chosen from the toolbar by clicking on the 'T' icon.

2. **Add Text:** Click on your video and create a text layer. Type whatever you like, then change font, size, and color in the Character and Paragraph panels.

3. **Editing Timings:** In the timeline, start adjusting the start and end points to control the time of this text appearing and disappearing in the video.

4. **Animate Text** (Optional): If you want to animate your text highlight in the timeline, the Toggle Animation icon, to the right of a property that you want to animate, such as the Opacity, Position, or Style.

Step 6: Adding Filters and Effects

Photoshop has a load of different filters that are part of the application that you can apply to your video layers for a stylized effect.

1. **Convert Video Layer for Smart Filters:** Right-click the **'Video'** layer and select **'Convert to Smart Object'** before adding filters. This smart object now will let you add filters to your video without its destruction.

2. Select Filter: Go to **Filter > Filter Gallery**, after which a vast variety of filters will be available, such as Gaussian Blur, Noise, Sharpen, etc. Each filter has different options for customizable effects.

3. **Adjusting the Effect:** You can modify the filter's setting by visiting the Properties panel. The smart filters allow you to edit or discard the effect at any time.

Step 7: Add Transitions and Animations

The transition and animation will help give your video smoothness and creativity.

1. **Add Transitions Between Clips**: In the timeline, click on the little transition icon. This opens a new window with options such as Fade, CrossFade, and Wipe. Then, take any one of these transitions and drop it on the start or end of any layer.

2. **Animate Properties**: To create an animation for properties like Position or Opacity, click the **Toggle Animation icon** next to the property in the timeline. Move the playhead to another point in time and adjust the settings of the property to create an animation keyframe.

Step 8: Previewing Your Edits

Before exporting, take a moment to play your work in the timeline, paying close attention to areas where you may want to make adjustments in timing, transitions, and effects.

Step 9: Exporting Your Video

If satisfied with the video, then it is time to export it.

1. **Export Settings**: After making all the changes and edits, go to File > Export > Render Video. A Render Video dialog box will pop up where you can choose the file name, location, format, and quality.

2. **Select the Format and Preset:** Within the Format, choose between H. 264 for MP4 and QuickTime for MOV. In Presets, you can select any from the pre-defined resolution/frame rate or do that on your own.

3. **Render the Video:** Click **Render** after going through your settings. These will now be exported, which may take some time depending on how big and complex your project is.

Step 10: Reviewing and Sharing Your Video

- After exporting, locate your video file and play it through to ensure that everything shows up as it should. You can now send, transfer, and share the edited video with family, friends, or on social media.

PREVIEW YOUR DOCUMENT ON A VIDEO MONITOR

Previewing an Adobe Photoshop 2025 document on a video monitor helps ensure that high-definition visuals are colored and laid out properly for the distribution of professional media content.

Step 1: Set up the Video Monitor

To get started with previewing your document on an external video monitor, connect it properly to your computer. For better results, connect using an HDMI or DisplayPort cable because these types of connections give high-definition video quality.

To do so;

1. **Connect the cable:** Connect the cable by using the HDMI or DisplayPort port available on your computer or graphics card and then hook it into the corresponding port on your video monitor.

2. **Turn on the monitor**: Power up your video monitor and ensure it is receiving a signal from your computer.

3. **Adjust display settings**: On your computer, go to **Settings > Display** (Windows) or **System Preferences > Displays** (Mac). Ensure the video monitor is set up as a secondary display or mirror your main screen if desired.

If you are working in Adobe Photoshop 2025 on either a laptop or desktop with multiple monitors, first determine which of your monitors is going to be your main display and which is your preview monitor. For ease of use, Adobe Photoshop recommends having your video monitor right next to your editing screen so images can be easily compared.

Step 2: Open Adobe Photoshop 2025 and Prepare Your Document

Open Adobe Photoshop 2025 after setting up your video monitor. Then, load the document that you want to preview. Your document should possess the appropriate resolution and color, depending on the display size and quality of the video monitor.

1. **Resolution settings:** Depending on the display size and quality of the video monitor, set your document to 1920 × 1080 pixels for HD monitors and 3840x2160 pixels for 4K monitors.

2. **Color mode**: For video display, choose RGB color mode which is the same as how monitors display color. Use sRGB document color for web and online, Rec. 709 for broadcast.

Step 3: Activating the Preview Feature

The Preview feature in Photoshop 2025 is greatly capable of having you tightly estimate your work on a video monitor. To activate the preview feature in Photoshop, follow these steps:

1. Go to **Window > Arrange**, and click **New Window** for [Your Document Name]. This will open another view of your open document that you can drag onto your video monitor.

2. Drag the additional window view onto the video monitor.

3. Now, go into **View > Proof Setup**, and choose **Monitor RGB** to show the correct color preview on the external monitor.

The idea is that you can edit your document on the main screen and make some observations there in real time on the video monitor, it could be a good reference for color accuracy and layout.

Step 4: Calibration of Color Settings for Accurate Representation

Accurate color representation on the video monitor is critical, especially in professional work. Here is how to adjust your color settings:

1. **Calibrate the monitor:** Most professional monitors will support hardware calibration. Look to the instructions for your monitor to do this.

2. **Photoshop color settings:** Go to **Edit > Color Settings** and check a color profile that matches your monitor's calibration - if in doubt, use sRGB or Adobe RGB.

3. **Proofing setup:** If working on projects for broadcast or video, select **View > Proof Setup > Custom** and choose a color profile such as **Rec. 709** to view what your document would look like when viewed on different screens of video.

Working with a calibrated monitor and correctly setting color profiles in the display settings of your computer can help you avoid unwanted color shifts when your work is viewed on another screen.

Step 5: Adjust Zoom Levels and Display Options

This video monitor might have different display settings compared to this main screen. Optimize your view to get the most accurate assessment of it. To do so,

1. **Setup zoom level:** This is an indication to choose a zoom level of 100% in Photoshop on the video monitor for accurate details of depictions at actual size.

2. **Full screen**: In the View menu, select **Fit Screen** or press **Ctrl+0** for Windows and **Command+0** for Mac to display your work in full screen. This is useful when one wants to view the entire document on a big screen.

3. **Toggle views:** Compare what your document will look like on and off the screen by clicking F to toggle between standard, full screen with menu bar, and full screen. This helps you see how your work might look under the wildly differing conditions it will be viewed.

Step 6: Fine-Tune Display Settings for Different Lighting Conditions

It can also teach a lot about brightness and contrast when viewing your document on a video monitor under various lighting conditions. To manipulate lighting, do the following:

1. **Adjust the room lighting**: You can minimize glare and ambient lighting that interfere with color perception. Soft-controlled lighting works best for an accurate preview.

2. **Adjust with Photoshop's Brightness/Contrast tools**: Go to **Image > Adjustments > Brightness/Contrast** to make any necessary adjustments to your image.

3. **View on different monitors**: When possible, view your document on other monitors to see how the differences in lighting alter what you can see.

This will be especially helpful when working in print design or video editing, as this will enable the designer to ensure colors are consistent over various devices.

Step 7: View Specific File Types for Video Production

Working on Photoshop documents intended for video takes a lot of confirmation regarding compatibility and quality of output. Correspondingly, Photoshop 2025 allows you to preview certain formats with the following features incorporated:

1. **Verify Export settings:** Go to **File > Export > Export As** and select the format you want to export your document in, such as JPEG, PNG, TIFF, MP4, etc.

2. **Use Timeline for movie files:** If your project includes animation or time-based media, choose **Window > Timeline** to reveal the Timeline panel so you can test the motion and effects playback right on the video monitor.

3. **Experiment with varying bit depth:** Once you have designed your composition, use **Image > Mode** to switch to 8-, 16-, or 32-bit color for smooth gradients and expanded dynamic range on high-end monitors.

Step 8: Test Performance and Make Final Tweaks

Once your document looks right on the screen, double-check your layout for any final edits. Consider the following elements to ensure a professional appearance and feel in your final document:

1. **Align and justify:** You may notice, now that you are proofing your layout on the larger video screen, some spacing and alignment problems.

2. **Check color consistency:** Go through your document and evaluate colors for any inconsistencies that do not match your color palette.

3. **Save and check within a video editor**: Export your Photoshop document into a video editor, such as Adobe Premiere Pro, to make sure compatibility is good and that the visual integrity holds.

TIMELINE ANIMATION WORKFLOW

Adobe Photoshop 2025 extends this timeline animation capability, giving more flexibility to the animator, designer, and creator. The essence of animation in Photoshop 2025 relies on the creation of a timeline, frame management or keyframe management, and layering for organization and customization of the workflow.

Step 1: Setting Up Your Document for Animation

Begin by setting up your document in such a way as to optimize it for animation.

1. **Create a New Document**: Open the menu **File > New** and set the dimensions of the document according to your needs. For online use, the normal size is 1080x1080 or 1920x1080 pixels, but for other platforms or some specific animation, you need to adjust its size. Set resolution to 72 dpi for web and screen display, and color mode to RGB.

2. **Activate Timeline**: Open the Window and then select **Timeline**. It will open a panel at the bottom that will enable you to set the frames or keyframes for your animation.

3. **Determine the Type of Animation**: Photoshop has two major kinds of animation:

   - **Frame Animation**: It is used to give traditional, frame-by-frame animations.
   - **Timeline Animation**: This is keyframe-based animation, and it works well for smooth and gradual transitions.

Timeline Animation is a first choice in most modern animations due to its great flexibility and smoother motion.

Step 2: Creating Layers for Animated Elements

Photoshop animations are essentially based on the manipulation of layers.

1. **Organize Your Layers**: Separate every element you would like to animate onto its layer. At this point, name your layers descriptively in your Layers panel to keep your workspace tidy: "**Background,**" "**Character,**" "**Text**".".

2. **Convert Layers for Smart Animation**: If you want to animate an object that requires any transformations such as scaling, rotating, or moving, it is best you convert it into a Smart Object. Right-click on the layer and select **'Convert to Smart Object'**. Smart objects

preserve the quality of your images when resizing or transforming and most importantly allow non-destructive editing.

Step 3: Creating the Animation in Timeline Mode

With the Timeline panel opened and your layers set, you are ready to animate.

1. **Add a Timeline Animation**: Click within the Timeline panel the button Create Video Timeline. Photoshop will instantly open a timeline and place each layer in its row, preparing it for keyframes.

2. **Set Animation Length**: Adjust the animation duration by using the length on the Timeline. You can drag the end of the timeline slider or set a time by clicking the time display at the bottom of the timeline.

3. **Choose a Frame Rate**: The number of frames per second, as defined by the frame rate, dictates the smoothness of your animation. For web and most animations, you want to be at 24-30 frames per second. Change this in **Timeline Options > Set Timeline Frame Rate**.

Step 4: Adding Keyframes

In any timeline animation, the keyframes are important, as they define points of change for your layers.

1. **Select Layer to Animate**: Click the arrow next to the layer name in the timeline to open a set of transform options, which include Position, Opacity, and Style.

2. **Setting Keyframes**: To set a keyframe, click the little stopwatch icon next to the property to which you want to add an animation. Doing so will set a keyframe at the current playhead position in the timeline.

3. **Keyframe Layer Properties Adjustment**: After having set the playhead at a different point in the timeline, adjust that property of the layer, for example - move position, and modify opacity. The adjustment will immediately open up Photoshop and create a new keyframe with these adjustments.

For example, to have an object move from left to right, you would create a keyframe for the beginning position of the object, then move the playhead to a point further along the timeline, and reposition the object on the canvas. Photoshop interpolates motion between these points to create a smooth transition.

Step 5: Refining Animation with Easing and Layer Styles

Adding easing and layer styles can help create a polished, professional look.

1. **Adding Ease to Keyframes**: Easing controls how much the speed of the transition between keyframes is accelerated or decelerated.

To add easing, right-click on any keyframe and select **Keyframe Assistant** to choose from such options as Ease In, Ease Out, or Ease In and Out.

2. **Animating Layer Styles**: To animate something like layer styles-shadows or glows-just add a keyframe for layer style where you want it in the timeline, double-click the little triangle icon that comes up, and change your style settings at different keyframes to show dynamic effects.

Step 6: Apply Transformations and Filters

Photoshop offers several transformations and filters that you can apply to extend your animation.

1. **Transform Animations:** Rotation, scale, and perspective with time can be done using the Free Transform tool under **Ctrl+T or Command+T**. You can introduce keyframes at the start and at the end of the zoom to bring attention to a specific area of the frame.

2. **Animating with Filters**: Apply filters as Smart Filters onto a Smart Object layer so that the filter effect can be animated. For example, the Blur filter can be animated to make objects appear in and out of focus.

Step 7: Previewing and Refining the Animation

Regularly previewing your animation ensures that transitions are smooth and any issues are identified at an early stage.

1. **Previewing the Animation**: The **Play button** in the Timeline panel is used to preview an animation. You can render the animation for a smoother preview by selecting **Render Video from the Timeline Options**.

2. **Adjust Timing:** If the movements of objects or characters feel too fast or too slow, adjust the spacing between the keyframes or drag the keyframes across the timeline, which changes the timing.

3. **Add Additional Effects**: Layer adjustments can also be made, such as the addition of adjustment layers or masks that can enhance the three-dimensional aspects of your animation.

Step 8: Adding Audio (Optional)

If your animation requires audio, Photoshop does support adding and synchronizing sound.

1. **Add Audio:** To add audio, simply go into **Layer > Audio > Add Audio** and select the audio file of your choice. The audio track will then appear in the Timeline panel, where you can edit and sync the audio with the animation.

2. **Audio Timing Editing**: You can trim the audio to perfectly align it with certain points of animation.

Step 9: Export Your Animation

If you are satisfied with your animated video, then export it.

1. **Export as GIF**: If your animation is very simple and for web usage only, then go to **File > Export > Save for Web** (Legacy); select GIF format, and adjust the settings to optimize the file size.

2. **Export as Video**: For high-quality animation export, head to **File > Export > Render Video;** select settings such as H.264 for web-compatible videos, with changed resolution and frame rate according to your needs. Now you have to name the file, locate it, and click Render.

SELECT INTERPOLATION METHOD

Understanding Interpolation in Photoshop

Interpolation in Photoshop refers to the process used in changing the pixel data when one resizes an image; it can upscale large or downscale it. What happens with this is that new pixels get added or discarded according to the interpolation method used in Photoshop. Clarity, sharpness, and overall quality of the image are influenced in such ways.

There exist a few interpolation options in Photoshop 2025, targeted for different types of resizing and other image contents. The appropriate selection of methods is very important because incorrect interpolations may result in undesirable artifacts or loss of detail.

Step 1: Entering Interpolation Settings

To select an interpolation method in Photoshop 2025, the following are the steps which you have to follow:

1. **Open the Image**: First of all, open the image which you intend to resize.

2. **Open Image Size Dialog Box**: Go to the top menu, then Image, and select **Image Size** to pop up the Image Size dialogue box, which holds the interpolation settings.

3. **Choose Resampling Method**: In the Image Size dialog, find the option that says Resample. Click on that to open the drop-down for selecting the interpolation method you want to apply.

Step 2: Understanding Interpolation Methods

With Adobe Photoshop 2025, there are a few different interpolation methods available, each fit for different resizing needs. A deeper look into each method looks something like this:

1. **Nearest Neighbor**
   - **Purpose**: Very simple and fast; it is mainly used for graphics that have hard edges.

- **Best For:** Pixel art, icons, and images with no smooth transitions.
- **Description**: Nearest Neighbor interpolation simply finds the nearest pixel and merely repeats its color value to populate new pixels. It doesn't introduce any new colors, which means it keeps the hard edges but results in blocky enlargement.

2. **Bilinear**
   - **Purpose**: Slightly smoother than the Nearest Neighbor, Bilinear is a basic method suitable for slight resizing.
   - **Best For:** Small adjustments where image quality isn't critical.
   - **Description**: There is a description with the color values of neighboring pixels taken into consideration for a softer transition in bilinear interpolation; this may introduce slight blurring. It is generally faster compared to other methods and may not deliver the best quality for high-resolution images.

3. **Bicubic**
   - **Purpose**: General-purpose interpolation for moderate resizing needs.
   - **Best For**: Photos and general images that need a good balance between smoothness and sharpness.
   - **Description**: Bicubic interpolation calculates new pixel values by taking the average of a block of pixels that surrounds it. Bicubic provides a much smoother and more natural appearance than either Nearest Neighbor or Bilinear and provides good quality for moderately sized resizing.

4. **Bicubic Smoother (Enlargement)**
   - **Purpose**: Best used when increasing image size.
   - **Best For**: Low-resolution images that need to be scaled up.
   - **Description**: Smoothness is important with Bicubic Smoother, and hence most of the noise and other unwanted stuff is reduced when you try to enlarge an image. This is good to go when images are small and you want to enlarge them, or you want them soft and natural looking. The only problem is that some details might be lost while doing this.

5. **Bicubic Sharper (Reduction)**
   - **Purpose**: Optimized to diminish the size of an image.
   - **Best For**: Large images that need to be downscaled and must not lose their sharpness.
   - **Description**: Bicubic Sharper intends to keep the details of the image sharp when downsizing. This resampling doesn't blur and is excellent in terms of clarity. This may, however, introduce unwanted noises or halos around the edges when this resampling is done to a higher extent.

Step 4: Choosing the Right Method for Your Image

While selecting the best interpolation method, consider these factors:

- **Image Type**: High-detail images, such as portraits, would greatly benefit from Preserve Details 2.0, while pixel art will look best with Nearest Neighbor.

- **Resizing Direction**: If you're increasing it, use Bicubic Smoother or Preserve Details 2.0. If you're decreasing it, use Bicubic Sharper.

- **Processing Power**: Techniques like Preserve Details 2.0 are superior and require more resources. Choose accordingly.

Step 5: Apply and Refine Resizing

1. **Enter the Desired Dimension**: In the Image Size dialog box, specify the width and height of your picture.

2. **Review Resample Settings**: Check whether the interpolation method, applied by default when resizing, will do the work or not.

3. **Preview the Result:** Photoshop has the preview option. With this option, one can zoom in to check defects or loss of any detail.

Step 6: Fine-Tuning with Smart Sharpen or Noise Reduction (Optional)

Sometimes, certain pictures might require sharpening or noise reduction after resizing. The following in Photoshop 2025 will help enhance the final result: sharpening and noise reduction.

1. **Sharpen**: Go to **Filter > Sharpen > Smart Sharpen** and refine the edges to get some clarity restored.

2. **Noise Reduction**: Open **Filter > Noise > Reduce Noise** to get rid of all the unwanted artifacts that could have been created by resizing.

Step 7: Saving the Resized Image

1. **Save as New**: Save the resized image, keeping the original intact, by going to the menu **File > Save As**.

2. **File Format**: Select the format you want. Web standard - JPEG and PNG; for print, use TIFF or high-quality JPEG.

3. **Adjust Compression**: When saving in the JPEG format, this lets you move the quality slider to balance the file size against quality.

COPY, PASTE, AND DELETE KEYFRAMES

Setting Up Keyframes in Adobe Photoshop 2025

Before copying or pasting keyframes and deleting them, ensure that you have keyframes to begin with. These mark the specific moment in your animation; thus, they define changes in layer properties, position, opacity, or style. To begin with, follow these steps:

1. **Open Timeline:** Open the timeline panel by going to **Window > Timeline**.

2. **Convert Layer for Animation:** Right-click on the layer to which you want to apply animation and select **Convert to Smart Object** so you can enable more editing on the timeline.

3. **Create Animation:** If you haven't already, click **Create Frame Animation** in the timeline panel. A new timeline for the layer will be created by Photoshop.

4. **Enable Keyframes for Properties**: On the timeline, next to the layer, click the small arrow; this will pop out properties, such as Position, Opacity, and Style. Next to each property, by clicking on the stopwatch icon, keyframes will be turned on.

Copying Keyframes

Copying keyframes is a good procedure to have similar animation effects uniformly implemented in parts of the timeline. Rather than having to create the animations from scratch, keyframes make things a bit easier. To copy keyframes in After Effects, follow these steps:

1. **Choose Keyframes**: Highlight the first keyframe you want to copy, by clicking on it in the timeline panel. To choose more than one, hold down Shift and click other keyframes.

2. **Right-click and Copy**: Do this while one of the keyframes is still selected or hit Ctrl+C for quick copying on Windows or Cmd+C on Mac.

3. **Choose Destination Layer and Frame**: Proceed with the timeline to the precise point when you would like the copied keyframes to have an effect. In case of copying on a different layer, tap the target layer on the timeline.

4. **Paste Keyframes**: Right-click anywhere in the timeline where you want to paste and select **Paste Keyframes** or use Ctrl+V for Windows or Cmd+V for Mac. The keyframes will then appear at the selected point in the timeline with the same properties and values as that of the original keyframes.

Adjusting Pasted Keyframes

After pasting, you may want to make minor adjustments to fit the effect you are trying to achieve. This step makes sure that the copied keyframes work seamlessly in your animation.

1. **Move Keyframes**: To adjust timing, drag each pasted keyframe left or right along the timeline.

2. **Edit Keyframe Properties**: For small changes of value continuities like opacity or position, click into every pasted keyframe to access the settings of its properties.

3. **Preview Animation:** Click the **Play button** on the timeline panel and look at the redeveloped animation to make sure that the keyframes that you copied create the desired effect.

Deleting Keyframes

If some keyframes are no longer needed in your animation, you can remove them to clean up the timeline and avoid useless frames being rendered. Here's how to remove keyframes:

1. **Choose Keyframes:** You can select a keyframe simply by clicking on it in the timeline. To delete many, you hold the **Shift key** while clicking other keyframes.

2. **Use Right-Click to Delete**: Right-clicking any selected keyframe will pop up a context menu from which you choose **Delete Keyframes**. It deletes selected keyframes, leaving the rest of the animation intact.

3. **Playback Confirmation**: After deletion, the playback on the animation needs to be checked. It must still flow as it is required to. Most of the time, keyframes around that area need to be adjusted to make it smooth.

Organizing Keyframes

As the animations gain in complexity, the organization of keyframes is pretty important. Here are a few tips to manage keyframes efficiently in Photoshop 2025:

1. **Timeline Navigation**: The Zoom slider at the bottom of the timeline allows you to see more frames or to focus closely on some frames.

   This makes it much easier when you need to select and manage keyframes.

2. **Group by Layer:** Sometimes, many items are placed in an animation, so it's easier to separate them into layers.

   Additionally, you may group related layers into folders for quick finding and editing of some keyframes.

3. **Label Keyframes:** Although labeling of keyframes isn't directly possible in Photoshop, you can achieve a visible structure within your project by using the naming convention for layers and color coding.

Troubleshooting Common Issues

With keyframes, sometimes, some issues may arise accidentally, such as keyframes not appearing after pasting, or an animation not playing correctly. Here are a few common problems along with their respective solutions:

1. **Keyframes Not Pasting Correctly:** Make sure you've selected an exact frame in the timeline to which you want to paste keyframes. You can only paste keyframes into frames that would allow change to specific properties.

2. **Playback Issues**: If, for some reason, your animation is not playing the way you want it to, first check that your timeline settings are set for Loop Playback so you can continually replay the test. Make sure all of your layers are in the right position in the timeline.

3. **Keyframes out of Sync**: If it seems like your keyframes are out of sync, this is due to the simple fact that all keyframes were not selected before you copied them. The Copy and Paste functions need to be highly specific or it will cause a desync.

Save and Export Your Animation

Once you have made adjustments to keyframes, you're ready to save or export your animation. Here's how to do so:

1. **Save the Project File:** To save your project as a PSD file in Adobe Photoshop, go to **File > Save As.** This will retain all keyframes and layers for possible future editing.

2. **Exporting Animation:** After reaching the menu, click **File > Export > Save for Web** (Legacy); choose GIF as the file format and click Save after making the desired settings. For exporting videos, the route will be **File > Export > Render Video**, then choose your format and export the animation.

CREATING HAND-DRAWN ANIMATIONS

Step 1: Setup Your Environment

Before you get started, set up your working space to become animation-friendly.

1. **Open the Timeline Panel:** Go to **Window > Timeline**. This opens the timeline panel; this is important when one is doing frame-by-frame animation.

2. **Choose 'Create Frame Animation':** In the timeline panel, click on **Create Frame Animation**. This sets up your document to frame-by-frame animation mode-meaning, each frame will have some drawing or different stage in your animation.

3. **Resizing the Canvas:** The default of your canvas size is set to your desired output resolution, like HD at 1920 x 1080. To change this, go to **Image > Canvas Size**.

4. **Set Frame Rate:** Set a frame rate for the animation. A higher frame rate, such as 24 frames per second, will have the animation move smoother; however, since you are just starting, you can have it lower, such as 12 fps.

With your workspace set, you are ready to start building the frames of your animation.

Step 2: Create a Rough Animation

Before you do a detailed drawing, do a rough animation. This lets you roughly see the motion and timing.

1. **Draw First Frame**: Using any gray tone or light color, roughly draw your first frame of animation. This way, it will be easier for you to tell them apart from your final lines.

2. **Duplicate Frame:** Click the + button underneath the timeline panel, duplicate the first frame, and adjust for the second frame in your animation sequence.

3. **Draw Keyframes**: Pre-produce keyframes by drawing the major poses of the animation. If a character has to wave, for instance, draw the hand resting position as one key frame and the raised position of the hand as the second keyframe. The frames between keyframes are used to refine the smoothness of the movement.

4. **Adjust Frame Duration**: First, select any frame in the timeline and then adjust the time of every frame in seconds. This will allow you to maintain a good tempo by viewing how long each of your drawings will stay on.

When you feel satisfied with the rough motion, you are ready to add detail to each frame.

Step 3: Refine Your Drawings

Once the rough animation is in, begin cleaning up each frame. This means re-drawing over your roughs for smooth, clean lines.

1. **Create a New Layer for Clean Lines**: Create a new layer above your layer containing the sketch in each frame. This will be for your final line art so you can later turn off the rough sketches.

2. **Draw Clean Line Art**: Using a finer brush, trace over each of your sketches on the new layer, changing its size to achieve the desired thickness/thinness in your lines.

3. **Keep Each Frame on Separate Layers**: For tidiness, have each cleaned frame on its separate layer, and name them for example "**Frame 1 Clean**".

4. **Play the Animation**: Click the **Play button** in the timeline to see the animation. Make the necessary changes to enhance flow and timing.

Smoothening of every frame will make your final product perfect, even if it's a small piece of animation.

Step 4: Adding Colors and Shading [Optional]

Adding colors and shading to your animation adds depth to it, making it complete. You can skip this step if you want a black-and-white effect.

1. **Add Base Colors:** On a new layer underneath your clean line art layer for each frame, with a basic brush fill in the base colors, making sure to stay inside the lines.

2. **Clipping Masks for Shadows and Highlights**: When adding in shading, a new layer goes over the color layer and is set as a clipping mask; this will contain the shading within the colored areas.

3. **Frame-to-Frame Consistency:** The colors and shades should be in continuity. Little variation negates the continuity of the animation.

4. **Check Color/Shade Continuity:** Play your animation to make sure that color and shade are continuous.

Adding color may take a long time, but it adds an added level of polish and professional appeal to your animation.

Step 5: Refine the Timing of Frames and Play the Animation

Fine-tuning of the frame timing is crucial to give your animation a smooth, natural look.

1. **Adjust Frame Durations**: Tap on every frame in the timeline to adjust the duration. Usually, faster movements take shorter frame lengths, while slower movements are longer.

2. **Add Hold Frames**: In animations that have pauses, for example, a character holding some pose, you need to duplicate a frame and then set a longer duration for the hold.

3. **Test and Refine**: Play the animation several times to get a feel of the timing of the image. You might have to adjust the image accordingly to let the animation flow.

Refining the timing is often a very minor process, but it can make all the difference in how the animation feels.

Step 6: Add Effects and Backgrounds (Optional)

If you want to add that extra oomph, go ahead and add backgrounds and effects like motion lines.

1. **Create a Background Layer**: If you want a static background, place a background layer at the bottom of your animation frames. You can simply create a scene in Flash or import an image into Flash.

2. **Add Effects**: Effects that can make something appear to move, such as motion lines or blurs, can be added to highlight the fact that something is moving. This should be done on new layers to keep your flexibility.

3. **Adding Adjustment Layers for Continuity**: Add adjustment layers that are continuous with the frame effects. You can have a color overlay for the continuity of the color palette in your animation.

Remember, the effects should be subtle; too many of them will distract from the main animation.

Step 7: Export the Animation

Once you are through with your animation, you will export it in various formats to be used, such as in GIF or MP4 format.

1. **GIF Export:** For creating a looping, web-friendly animation, head over to File Export Save for Web Legacy, choose **GIF** as the format, and play with the settings until it feels right. If you want it to loop as one, continuous animation, make sure you check that box.

2. **Video Export:** For the more professional video format, go to **File > Export > Render Video**, and choose your favored video settings-resolution and frame rate among them.

3. **Change Export Settings**: Let your export setting be as close to the quality and file size you want. You can play with settings to get the best balance.

Exporting your work makes sure that you have, with you, a shareable version of your hand-drawn animation.

Step 8: Review and Share Your Animation

Lastly, review the animation to ensure it looks good on various devices, if you plan to share it online.

1. **Preview on Different Devices:** Observe the animation on the phone, tablet, or desktop to ensure the quality remains.

2. **Gather Feedback:** Share your animation with your peers or different animation communities to get constructive criticism.

3. **Share Your Work:** Upload your animation to different social media, portfolios, or publishing platforms for animation.

CHAPTER EIGHT

WORKING WITH FILTERS AND EFFECTS

USING LIVE GAUSSIAN BLUR FILTER

The Live Gaussian Blur filter in Adobe Photoshop 2025 (Beta) allows for non-destructive and dynamic blurring of parts of your image with the most control over the effect. Unlike traditional Gaussian blur, which forever changes the layer it's applied to, Live Gaussian Blur does not commit changes, and this enables real-time adjustments. Well, this is a feature that was developed in the Beta phase.

Step 1: Setting Up Your Workspace

1. **Open Adobe Photoshop 2025**: Ensure that you have installed the latest version. Click on the Photoshop menu, then go to **File > Open** to load your image.

2. **Create a Backup Layer (Optional):** You never know if you might want to go back to a previous image, so it's often good to work on a copy of your original image layer. To do this, right-click your background layer in the Layers panel, then click on **Duplicate Layer**. Make the duplicate layer's name identifiable, like **"Blur Layer."**

3. **Convert to Smart Object**: Right-click on the layer and choose **Convert to Smart Object**. This is an important step in Lightroom as the Live Gaussian Blur will be added as a Smart Filter-you can move the blur effect with no destructive action on the original image.

Step 2: Accessing the Live Gaussian Blur Filter

1. **Open the Filters Panel**: Reach the top menu bar and click **Filter > Blur > Live Gaussian Blur**. By default, this will add a live Gaussian blur effect to your layer as a Smart Filter, and the options panel for Live Gaussian Blur will pop right up.

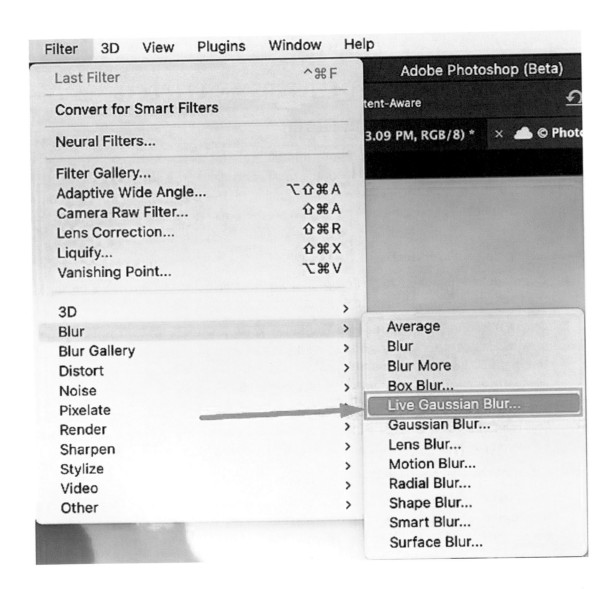

2. **Tour of the Live Gaussian Blur Interface**: The Live Gaussian Blur interface has a Radius slider and a Preview check box. The Radius slider is used to increase or decrease the intensity of the blur, whereas the Preview checkbox toggles whether you can see the blur applied as you are applying it.

Step 3: Set the Desired Blur by adjusting the radius

1. **Adjust Radius Slider**: In the Live Gaussian Blur panel, move the slider right upwards for a more extreme blur. The radius simply controls how far the blur spreads across the pixels of your image; therefore, the bigger its value, the more it becomes apparent.

Gaussian Blur

Blur Amount   20.0 px

Fade Opacity   100%

Output: New Layer

☑ Preview   (Cancel)   (OK)

2. **Preview the Effect:** Put a checkmark in the box beside Preview so you can view your effect as you go. Now, take the radius to the right until you reach an amount of blur that meets your artistic needs for the picture. You will probably want to stay between 5-15 pixels for the blur in subtle background blurs and much higher for dramatic effects.

3. **Focus on Key Areas (If Applicable)**: Where in the image would you like to draw the viewer's attention to? Remember, since Live Gaussian Blur is non-destructive, you will be able to mask parts of it later on, which will show you quite dramatic control over focus.

Step 4: Using the Mask to Apply Blur Selectively

1. **Add a Mask to the Smart Filter**: Once you've added the initial blur, notice that a mask thumbnail has appeared next to the Live Gaussian Blur in the Layer panel. Click the mask thumbnail to ensure it's active.

2. **Paint Over Areas for Adjusting Blur:** With the Brush Tool select paint over areas where you want to control the intensity of the blur. Since the mask is selected,
   - **Black** will mask the blur effect in specific areas.
   - **White** will reveal a full blur.
   - **Gray** shades will partially mask the blur, therefore allowing you to create a gradual transition.

3. **Adjust Brush Settings:** Choose a soft-edged brush to create smooth, natural transitions. You can change the size and opacity of the brush as you go. A low-opacity brush will apply subtle mask effects, while high opacity shows or hides the blur more aggressively.

4. **Play with the Layers' Opacity**: You can try making the mask more or less effective by changing the opacity of brush strokes or playing with gray shades.

Step 5: Refining the Blur by Further Adjustments

1. **Apply Multiple Live Gaussian Blur Layers**: If you want to add some depth, just duplicate this layer that contains the Smart Filter and for each of them the Radius. This makes for a layered type of blur effect where you could focus on an element in your frame by manipulating how sharp different elements will appear.

2. **Adjust Layer Blending Modes:** Combine the blurred layer with the original image using different modes of blending. The option to change the mode sometimes yields special lighting or textural effects to increase the apparent effect of the blur.

3. **Use Adjustment Layers for Extra Effects**: Add adjustment layers to adjust the brightness/contrast, and hue/saturation of this blurred area to offer a subtle variation that enhances the in-focus subject of your image. Make sure the adjustment layers are affecting only the blurred area by adding clipping masks or adjusting layer opacity as necessary.

Step 6: Checking and Refining the Final Effect

1. **Toggle the Live Gaussian Blur On and Off:** Click the eye icon next to the Smart Filter in the Layers panel to turn the Live Gaussian Blur effect on and off. Just a good way to see if the blur appears organic and working for you.

2. **Refine Radius if Necessary:** If at any time you do not like the strength of the blur, click back on the Live Gaussian Blur filter to adjust the Radius slider to fine-tune the amount of blur.

3. **Zoom In for Detail Work**: Zoom in to check areas that take detailed work, especially with edges and transitions, to ensure that the blurring does not look unnatural or rough.

Step 7: Exporting Your Image

1. **Save the File in PSD Format**: If you want to maintain all its editable layers, masks, and Smart Filters within your project.

2. **Export in Other Formats**: You can export a flattened version by going to **File > Export > Export As**, and then selecting your preferred format, such as JPEG or PNG. Make sure you follow proper export settings of quality, color space, and resolution.

3. **Check Final Quality:** After exporting the file, reopen it to make sure everything feels right. The blur should feel like it is supposed to, and it should improve and not hurt the subject of your image.

RESTORE NOISE IN BLURRED AREAS

Follow the steps below to restore noise in blurred areas:

Step 1: Duplicate the Layer

1. Open your image in Adobe Photoshop 2025.

2. In the Layers panel, right-click on your background layer, or the layer that contains your blurred image, and select **Duplicate Layer**. This will give us a duplicated layer with which we can work non-destructively and compare our changes.

3. To rename the duplicated layer to something descriptive like "**Noise Restoration Layer**," double-click on the name.

It is important to duplicate the layer because it will save the source image. Then, by working with a duplicated layer, if needed you may return to the source anytime when you're not satisfied with the result.

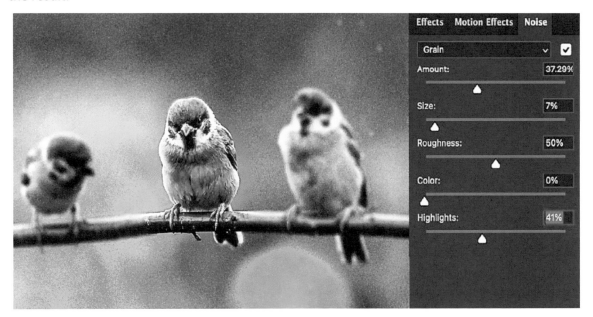

Step 2: Making a Selection of the Blurred Areas

1. Choose one of the selection tools in Photoshop, like the Quick Selection Tool or the Lasso Tool-whichever you feel is easiest for the area that needs a selection highlight those blurry areas where you want to restore noise.

2. Carefully overpaint or paint in the foggy areas of the image. For finer selections, try using Select and Mask under the Select menu. You can refine edges there, feather it, and get a much more organic selection.

Time needs to be taken with this selection because this is going to define where the noise is restored. This ensures that the added noise affects only what is intended.

Step 3: Refined Selection with Feathering

1. Once the selection is made, click on **Select > Modify > Feather**.

2. Give it a small feather radius, between 2 to 5 pixels depending on your image resolution. Feathering will help in blending the noise effect smoothly into the surrounding pixels and not create harsh lines where the effect begins and ends.

This enables feathering to make the transition between them almost invisible since the blurred area in most instances blends into the remainder of the image.

Step 4: Apply a Noise Filter to the Selection

1. Click **Filter > Noise > Add Noise**.
2. In the Add Noise dialogue box, you will have a set of options that you can apply to develop your noise feature:
   - **Amount**: This controls the intensity of the noise. A range of 5-10% is generally good for the slightly blurred regions, but of course, you might get more if it is strongly blurred.
   - **Distribution**: There is an option to choose either Uniform or Gaussian distribution of noise. The former often turns out more natural, though sometimes it might look just a bit more artificial.
   - **Monochromatic**: This checks if you just want pure black-and-white noise. Very good to go for grayscale images, or if you don't want colored distortions. If you want colored noise, uncheck this.

Apply the noise, and within that selection area, you should start seeing a little grain. If you need to, make further adjustments to the amount until you get the right texture.

Step 5: Apply a Gaussian Blur to the Noise (Optional)

1. To slightly mellow this noise effect, go to **Filter > Blur > Gaussian Blur**.

2. In the Gaussian Blur dialog, select a very low radius. This step adds some smoothness to the noise so that it does not look too sharp or unnatural.

Applying the Gaussian Blur will be more effective in regions with larger, smoother blurred portions because sharp noise tends to look unnatural there.

Step 6: Adding a Layer Mask for Detail (Optional)

1. If you want more detail about where the noise will and won't appear, click the mask icon in the Layers panel to add a Layer Mask.

2. Having selected the Brush Tool, set its opacity to some 50%, and on the layer mask, paint over areas where you want the noise effect to be hidden. You will hide the effect by painting with black color and revealing it by painting with white.

A layer mask can allow refining the application of noise further in case you need to avoid small details that don't require noise.

Step 7: Refine the Noise with the Layer's Opacity

1. If the noise effect still feels a bit too strong or too subtle, this can be subtly refined by adjusting the Opacity of the Noise Restoration Layer.

2. Just slightly lower the opacity to, for example, 70-80% for a balanced realistic look. This might be helpful in case the noise overpowers the natural look of the image.

A non-destructive means of adjusting the extent of the noise comes through the use of the layer's opacity.

Step 8: Add Additional Noise to Better Replicate the Original Image (if Needed)

1. If your image had different levels of noise originally, you may want to make an added layer of noise to better replicate it.

2. For this step, create a new layer and fill it with 50% gray by selecting **Edit > Fill** and choosing 50% gray from the dropdown menu.

3. Set this new layer mode to Overlay.

4. Then go to **Filter > Noise > Add Noise** and set the amount according to your image. You can add Gaussian Blur here too to blend it naturally.

This step works perfectly for those images in which the noise was there but it has been removed by blurring.

Step 9: Review and Refine

1. Merge a View of your image to **100%** or larger and ensure the noisy effect sits well.

2. If some areas show too sharp noise or even appear to be misplaced, go back into your layer mask and clean up using the Brush Tool for better results.

The time taken in refining will pay off when you get a professional and eye-catching output.

Step 10: Save Your Work

1. When you are satisfied with the noise restoration, save your work: Navigate to **File > Save As** and save it as a Photoshop PSD to retain all of your layers and masks.

2. Export a flattened version in a format of your choice, such as JPEG or PNG, if you need to do so for easier sharing.

Save a layered version so you can revisit and make changes at a later date if you so wish.

APPLY THE LIGHTING EFFECTS FILTER

Step 1: Preparing Your Image

1. **Open Your Image**: First, open Adobe Photoshop 2025 and then go to File > Open to choose the image you want to edit.

2. **Duplicate the Layer**: Since you want the original image intact, you will have to duplicate your background layer by hitting **Ctrl+J for Windows** or **Cmd+J for Mac**. This duplication allows for any edits non-destructively.

3. **Convert the Layer into a Smart Object**: You right-click on the duplicated layer and then convert it to a Smart Object. This step works advantageously in that you can go back and re-edit the lighting effects without having to alter the layer destructively.

Step 2: Access Lighting Effects Filter

1. **Open the Filter Menu**: On the top menu select **Filter > Render > Lighting Effects**. It opens a workspace called Lighting Effects that provides several options along with controls.

2. **Setup Your Workspace**: After opening the workspace in Lighting Effects, your image will load up the center screen with a default overlay of a light source that you can move and resize, as well as a property panel on the right-hand side of the workspace. This will be all you need to conduct any type of lighting effects.

Step 3: Choose a Light Type

Inside the Lighting Effects filter in Photoshop, there are several types of light sources with which you can work. Each of these produces something different:

1. **Spotlight**: It is the most versatile and will, in most cases, be applied to point out a section of the image by focusing a light beam on a particular area of the image. It's good for dramatic emphasis.

2. **Point Light:** Emulates the action of a light bulb in casting light in every direction from a central point. This works well in the creation of overall illumination.

3. **Infinite Light:** Will imitate sunlight or any other light that comes from far away, casting even light across the entire image.

4. **Adjust Light Position:** Click and drag in the preview window to reposition the light source by tugging it. Dragging at different angles until the best fit for your image is accomplished.

Step 4: Refine Light Properties

Refine the properties for the perfect look once you have selected a light type.

1. **Light Color**: From here, you can choose the color of your light from the properties panel. You will see a color swatch here on the right. Opening the color picker will allow you to pick any color. You can pick colors of a warm shade to add warmth to your image. You can also use a cool color to make things more dramatic or nighttime feel.

2. **Intensity**: The Intensity slider controls the brightness of your light source. Higher intensities cast more illumination, while lower intensities yield a subtle effect.

3. **Hotspot (Only for Spotlights):** The Hotspot slider controls the center brightness of the spotlight. The higher the value set for Hotspot, the stronger the beam in the middle of the light will be.

Step 5: Refine Lighting Size and Angle Control

With Photoshop 2025, you'll be able to adjust anything-from the shape to spread, to the angle of every light in your lighting effects.

1. **Shape and Spread**: Drag the outer handles of the light to resize. For a Spotlight, this will also be a change of shape. The larger the shape the more spread out the light will be; the smaller the shape the tighter the beam.

2. **Light Angle Rotation**: Drag the rotation handle circling the light source to adjust its angle. Rotating light enables you to send your shadows and highlights to accentuate parts of your image.

Step 6: Refining Texture and Ambiance

The Lighting Effects filter allows you to make more intricate adjustments that will help make your image pop.

1. **Ambiance**: The overall lightness or darkness in the background of the image should be selected by using the Ambient slider in the properties panel. Higher values of ambient light may soften the light whereas smaller values may make the scene more dramatic.

2. **Texture Channel**: Photoshop 2025 lets you add a texture channel to your light source. This will be very useful for those images which have distinct textures, such as fabrics, rocks, and wood. Click the drop-down menu to select a texture channel and use the Height slider to show how much of the texture you want. The bigger the number, the more pronounced the texture will be.

Step 7: Playing with Multiple Lights

Complex lighting is achieved by using multiple light sources to do so:

1. **Extra Lights**: To add an extra light, click on the New button in the properties panel. Each light can be adjusted for its type, color, and intensity independent of the other lights.

2. **Lighting Composites:** Experiment with combining light types, like a hot spot from a Spotlight combined with the general fill lighting from a Point Light. The layering of multiple lights adds depth to an image.

Step 8: Shadow Preview and Manipulation

Lighting Effects can be used to create realistic shadows that add even more reality to an image.

1. **Shadow Controls:** Under the properties panel, there is a slider labeled as Shadow. This controls how light or strong your shadows from your lighting are.

2. **Placement of Shadows:** The placement of your shadows can be changed by simply moving your light around and changing the angles. You will find with some playing around that it may feel most natural at one particular angle.

Step 9: Finishing the Lighting Effect

Now that you have set all of the adjustments for your lighting, it's time to finalize your image.

1. **Before and After Preview:** Enable and disable the Lighting Effects layer in the Layers panel, to compare the original with the edited image.

2. **Apply the Effect:** Once all is set, click OK to apply the Lighting Effects to your image. If you have converted your layer into a Smart Object, you can go back and re-edit the lighting effects by double-clicking the Lighting Effects option under your Smart Object layer.

Step 10: Fine Tuning with Additional Adjustments

After the Lighting Effects filter, some other enhancements can be made to the image.

1. **Adjustment Layers**: Add Brightness/Contrast, Levels, or Curves adjustment layers to fine-tune the image. These will help improve the contrast or remove any unwanted color shifts that might have occurred due to the adjustment of the lighting.

2. **Layer Masks**: Apply layer masks to selectively apply the light effect to parts of your image.

WORK WITH THE OIL PAINT FILTER

The ordinary picture pops into a beautiful and amazing painting with the use of an Oil Paint filter in Adobe Photoshop 2025, rivaling the great masters of oil on canvas. This dynamic filter will work great while adding an artistic touch to portraits, landscapes, or other images, as the features of this effect make the image textured and uniquely hand-painted-looking.

Step 1: Preparing Your Image

1. **Open Your Image in Photoshop**: Start by opening an image you want to edit in Photoshop. Go to **File > Open** and select your file. If your image is low resolution, you may want to upscale it first by going to **Image > Image Size** to preserve detail and ensure a high-quality result.

2. **Convert the Layer to a Smart Object (Optional but Recommended):** Making your layer a Smart Object will let you apply the Oil Paint filter non-destructively-that is, you can come back anytime and adjust your filter settings by right-clicking on the image layer in the Layers panel and choosing **Convert to Smart Object.**

3. **Copying the Layer (Optional):** You want to duplicate the layer for comparison against your original image. You simply select a layer and press Ctrl + J for Windows or Cmd + J for Mac. Then click on the eye icon to hide the original layer so that you can only focus on the layer in which you apply the filter.

Step 2: Locate the Oil Paint Filter

1. **Go to the Filter Menu:** With your image layer selected, go to **Filter > Stylize > Oil Paint.** This will open the Oil Paint dialog box, where you'll find the various settings to help customize this effect.

2. **Understanding the Oil Paint Settings**

The Oil Paint filter includes several sliders that let you control the strength, texture, and lighting of the filter's results. Each slider has a different effect on your image, so take time to understand exactly what each does as you apply the filter:

- **Stylization**: This controls the refinement of brush strokes. The higher the value, the smoother and more refined it will look; the lower the value, the more detailed and textured it will be.
- **Cleanliness**: Controls the flow of the strokes and their uniformity. The higher the value set, the cleaner and less textured the image appears; the lower it is, the more texture and grit in the image give a better realism.
- **Scale**: It is the setting that determines the size of the brush stroke. A large-scale value naturally gives bold strokes, while a smaller-scale value yields an intricate, detailed effect.
- **Bristle Detail:** Controls the fineness of the strokes to provide the image with a sense of brush depth. Higher values increase texture, giving it a more rough look, while lower values smooth the effect.
- **Lighting**: Adds three-dimensionality to the brush strokes. Angle and Shine can be adjusted.

Step 3: Working with the Effect Oil Paint

1. **Adjust the Stylization Slider**: First, the Stylization slider sets the overall look of the painting. Play with this value to achieve a style that best suits your image; for portraits, often higher Stylization works well and gives a soft refined look. For landscapes, try lower Stylization for a textured detailed look.

2. **Adjust the Cleanliness Slider**: Move the Cleanliness slider upwards to render the brush strokes smooth and even. Move it down to introduce a grittier texture into the brushes. For portraits, moving the Cleanliness upwards can render an airbrushed look. In natural scenes, low Cleanliness can add depth to a piece and bring out textures of trees, water, or rocks.

3. **Set the Scale and Bristle Detail**
   - The Scale slider controls the size of the brush strokes. If you want large, bold brush strokes, increase the Scale. For smaller, finer strokes, decrease it. Larger strokes can be effective for bold, impressionistic effects, and smaller ones can yield detailed work that's especially good in close-up shots.
   - Bristle Detail adds texture by controlling the visible bristle pattern. The higher the value, the more the brush texture and depth are emphasized. This gives an image a more painterly and handmade feel. Lower values produce a more blended, smooth result.

4. **Lighting-Create a Three-Dimensional Effect**
   - **Angle**: This sets the direction of the lighting source. By adjusting this, you might get variance in shadow and highlights on the strokes which will add depth to the created strokes. Play with different angles to see which direction gives you the most natural feeling for your image.
   - **Shine**: This shows how much shine is applied to the brush strokes. The higher the Shine, the glossier it is and the three-dimensional effect. If one wants to give a more discrete look, then they can turn Shine down by setting it flatter and more matte.

Step 4: Refining the Effect

1. **Fine-tune the sliders**: Once you have moved all of the sliders, go back and readjust as necessary. As stated previously, the sliders interact with each other so changing one setting could affect the characteristics of another. Take your time to get the right balance, focusing on what the desired look is.

2. **Preview and Toggle the Effect**: Click the **Preview check box** in the Oil Paint dialog box to toggle the effect on and off, so that you can see how the original image without the effect compares to the edited image, to gauge whether you are happy with it.

3. **Apply the Filter:** Once you like the effect, click OK to apply the Oil Paint filter on your image. If you have converted your layer to a Smart Object earlier, it will show up as a Smart Filter, and double-clicking on it will open it again for editing.

Step 5: Enhancing Oil Paint Effect (Optional)

1. **Duplicate Oil Paint Layer to Increase Its Intensity**: To take it even further and achieve an even more extreme painterly effect, with the Oil Paint layer selected press Ctrl + J (Windows) or Cmd + J (Mac) to duplicate the layer. This lays the effect over itself, amplifying it. Move the Opacity of the duplicated layer until it achieves the strength desired.

2. **Add Additional Filters or Adjustments**

Take your oil-painted image to another level by adding extra filters or adjustment layers:

- **Brightness/Contrast:** This may give it a pop with colors; **Image > Adjustments > Brightness/Contrast**.
- **Hue/Saturation**: You can further fine-tune color tones using Hue/Saturation.
- **Texture Filters**: The Noise or Grain filters will add more texture.

3. **Sharpen for Extra Definition:** After applying the Oil Paint filter, you should consider adding some sharpening to bring out detail and enhance the texture further. To sharpen in a more controlled fashion, go to **Filter > Sharpen > Unsharp Mask** or **High Pass filter**.

Step 6: Saving Your Oil Painting Image

Save the masterpiece once you are pleased with it. To do this, go to **File > Save As** and choose the format that will serve you best-whether JPEG if you want to share it online, or PSD in case you want to keep the layers for further changes.

APPLYING THE LIQUIFY FILTER

Step 1: Opening the Liquify Filter

1. **Open your image**: First, open any image in Photoshop which you want to edit. The Liquify filter can be applied to every layer; however, if you want to leave your original image intact, you will need to duplicate your layer before proceeding by using Ctrl+J or Command+J.

2. **Access the Liquify filter**: Up on your screen, click on **Filter**, then click on **Liquify** from the pull-down menu. This opens the Liquify dialog box containing an array of tools and settings specific for reshaping, distorting, or enhancing elements in your photo.

Step 2: Understanding the Liquify Interface

The Liquify workspace has several key sections:

- **Toolbar**: This is on the left side, housing all the tools for warping and adjusting the image, which includes Forward Warping, Pucker, and Bloat, among others.

- **Properties panel**: On the right-hand side, the window contains adjustable sliders for each tool, including options for face-aware editing, brush size, pressure, and density.
- **Image preview**: The central space where you will view the changing results of your actions in real-time.

Familiarize yourself with this layout, as it will make navigation when working with the Liquify tools a great deal easier.

Step 3: Using the Face-Aware Liquify Feature

The Face-Aware Liquify feature in Photoshop 2025 is a great feature that makes adjusting facial features so much easier without having to manually reshape every element.

1. **Enable the Face-Aware Liquify Feature**: In the Properties panel, you will see the section entitled Face-Aware Liquify. The software will instantly detect faces in your image.

2. **Change Individual Features**: You will be given choices to modify your Eyes, Nose, Mouth, and Face Shape. In each category of facial features, you will be given options to adjust attributes like Eye Size, Eye Distance, Nose Height, Mouth Width, and Face Width. These controls will let you subtly enhance or morph the face to consideration of natural proportions.

3. **Symmetrical Settings:** During symmetrical adjustments, the Link icon needs to be on so that one side of the face is a perfect mirror of the other. During asymmetrical adjustments, the icon should be turned off to allow changes on each feature independently.

Step 4: Forward Warp Tool

The Forward Warp Tool is the most functional tool under the Liquify filter. You simply use it to push and pull pixels to redefine the shape of an image area.

1. **Choose Forward Warp Tool**: Get the Forward Warp Tool by pressing **W** in the toolbar. This is ideal for making generalized manipulations on the image about its shape and will most often be used just to nudge - or sometimes pull out - areas slightly to get that refined look.

2. **Adjust the Brush Settings:** To change the brush size, density, and pressure, use the Properties panel. Generally speaking, larger brush sizes will affect wider areas, with smaller brushes allowing more precise edits.

3. **Start Warping**: Click and drag across the area you want to distort. For example, subtly push in the edges of a waist or warp the shape of an eyebrow. What's great about the Forward Warp tool is making changes along the organic lines of your subject.

Step 5: Pucker and Bloat Tools

The Pucker and Bloat tools will let you shrink or expand parts of an image selectively.

1. **Pucker Tool (S):** Pulls the pixels inwards from the center towards the brush; in turn, this action decreases the size of the surface. It is good and will be used for refining small areas like the tip of the nose or to slim down.

2. **Bloat Tool (B):** Just the opposite, it pushes out the pixels, and with that action, it can create an enlargement effect. It works fine on the eyes or gives a bit more shape to the lips.

3. **Adjust Brush Settings:** De-select the Brush Size and Pressure will link with shrink or bloat amount as needed for subtlety or intensity.

Step 6: Reconstruct Tool

Reconstruct Tool (R) will allow you to revisit some areas of the image back to its original setting.

1. **Select Reconstruct Tool:** This is found under the toolbar. It's used when one has overdone an effect or if gradually bringing back an area into its original shape.

2. **Brush over area**: Just brush through areas of the image that you want to restore. The tool will bring back the original pixels by refining the area where one might have warped too much.

Step 7: Freeze and Thaw Masks

The Freeze and Thaw tools mask or shield parts of your image as you make edits. In simpler terms, it's used to protect any part of the image with a background or any other important details that you do not want to be affected.

1. **Choose the Freeze Mask Tool (F):** Click and drag over areas to be protected. This prevents the covered area from the use of other Liquify tools so that at least some of your image will remain intact.

2. **Choose the Thaw Mask Tool (D):** This tool unfreezes the frozen parts to make them editable again. Proceed to unfreeze the frozen parts where your change of mind did not protect an area.

Step 8: Saving and Applying Changes

1. **Preview your edits:** The Properties panel contains a Show Backdrop option that can be used to view an image before and after editing. It ensures that the changes you have made appear natural and part of the general composition.

2. **Click OK:** Once you feel satisfied with the edits that you have made, click OK to save the changes and return to the main workspace in Photoshop.

APPLY SPECIFIC FILTERS

Step 1: Preparing Your Image

1. **Open Your Image:** Open Adobe Photoshop 2025 and open your picture to work on by clicking on **File > Open**.

2. **Duplicate the Layer**: Then, duplicate the layer. It is always good to have your original image to go back to in case you want to compare results or make changes. To do this, right-click on the layer via the Layers panel and click on **Duplicate Layer**.

Step 2: Apply Basic Adjustment Filter

The Basic Adjustment filter is new in Photoshop 2025 and places basic color, brightness, and contrast tweaks under one interface roof.

1. **Open the Basic Adjustments Filter**: To do so, go to **Filter > Basic Adjustment**. This tool is a real-time-saver when editing because it provides several sliders in one menu.

2. **Adjust Brightness and Contrast**: Take these sliders and increase the brightness and contrast slightly to bring out details that may be shadowed without overexposing the highlights.

3. **Enhance Color Saturation:** Take the saturation up to make colors more vibrant. Care should be taken not to over-saturate the colors; that will make the image unnatural. Generally, increasing the saturation by about 10-15% would suffice for a reasonable effect.

4. **Modify Exposure:** If you need something more dramatic, then you may use an exposure slider. A minor increase in exposure helps improve the overall visibility of an image, especially those captured in low-light conditions.

Step 3: Apply Neural Filters

The Neural Filters in Photoshop 2025 have been updated to include options that are more subtle and AI-powered for operations such as Landscape Mixer and Harmonization.

1. **Open the Neural Filters**: Use the menu by going to **Filter > Neural Filters**. A Neural Filter window opens showing a list of options; each of them powered by AI for better accuracy and effects.

2. **Apply the Landscape Mixer**: If your image is a landscape, then select Landscape Mixer. By selecting this filter, you can change the time of day, season, and the weather that's in your image. You can now set up the sliders to make your scene warmer or cooler; add snow or a sunset. This is an awesome filter when it comes to mood change.

3. **Apply the Harmonization Filter:** The Harmonization filter will match the color scheme and lighting of one image to another. You can apply this if you want your image to match a particular theme or some other photograph's color tone.

4. **Refine the Output**: Use the available sliders to adjust the strength, color balance, and tone. Then click OK to save the changes and apply.

Step 4: Adding the Depth Blur Filter

The Depth Blur filter applies a camera-like blur to a selected portion of an image using Photoshop 2025.

1. **Open the Depth Blur:** Open it from the **Filter menu > Depth Blur**. This filter can also simulate depth of field and blur selected areas so that the main subject stands out.

2. **Adjust Focal Range:** Tap your screen to set the focal point within the image, where you want it to stay sharp. Then you need to adjust the focal range to get just the right amount of blur in the background that will guide the viewer's eye into the focal point.

3. **Refine Blur Intensity:** You can plus or minus the strength of the blur according to your needs. This would be very effective, especially in portrait and macro photography, to emphasize the subject.

4. **Add Bokeh Effects (Optional):** The Depth Blur filter also has a Bokeh option. With this, you will be able to add subtle or extreme circular highlights similar to those that would have been created by a camera lens.

Step 5: Applying the Stylize Filters

Stylized filters are great for creative, flashy effects.

1. Select the Filter Stylize: To access the Stylize filters select **Filter > Stylize** and select **Oil Paint** or **Emboss**.

2. **Apply the Oil Paint Filter:** Under the Oil Paint, if selected, move the Stylization and Cleanliness sliders to set the amount of smoothness and the appearance of brushstrokes. This will give an effect to your image of it being painted, which is ideal when trying to achieve an artistic effect.

3. **Use the Emboss Filter**: The Emboss filter applies a gray-scale texture that gives an image a 3D effect. It works well on textural images of rocks or fabrics. You will be able to adjust the direction and the intensity of the embossed effect by moving the Angle and Height sliders.

Step 6: Final Touches with Camera Raw Filter

The Camera Raw Filter is great for final adjustments in polishing your image.

1. **Open the Camera Raw Filter**: Go to **Filter > Camera Raw Filter**. It opens an advanced interface with detailed controls over color, contrast, clarity, and many more.

2. **Work with Shadows and Highlights**: You can make a good balance in the light distribution in your image by using the Shadows and Highlights sliders. Darkening the shadow will help you with depth while brightening the highlights will add liveliness.

3. **Add Clarity and Dehaze**: Give it more punch by slightly increasing clarity. Dehaze works effectively on outdoor images as it removes the haze factor resulting from natural elements, such as fog or mist.

4. **Refine Colors with Split Toning**: Split Toning will allow you to add color to the shadows and highlights. You can use it to give your image a colored grade effect, similar to film or movie shots.

Step 7: Saving and Export

Once satisfied with your edits, it's time to save your work.

1. **Save the Project**: Under the **File Menu,** select **Save As**; name and save your project as a PSD - this will give you all layers and adjustments if you would like to make edits later.

2. **Export the Image**: With **File > Export > Export As**, select a format you want to use with regards to your final image: JPEG, PNG, etc. Now under quality settings, choose from the dropdown menu high, medium, or low depending on whether one is printing out the image or putting it onto the web.

3. **Final Check:** Finally, double-check your picture at various zoom levels to make sure that minute details have not been taken care of and the entire image is cohesive and balanced.

CHAPTER NINE

TEXT, TYPOGRAPHY, AND DESIGN TOOLS

ADD OR PLACE TEXT

Step 1: Setting Up Your Canvas

1. **Open Photoshop and Create a New Document**: Open Adobe Photoshop 2025: open a new document via **File > New** or Ctrl+N on a PC. If you work on a Mac, then use the keyboard shortcut Cmd+N. You can choose here the size, resolution, and color mode of the whole canvas. For web use, it's RGB; for print, CMYK.

2. **Select Your Canvas Size:** Select your canvas size, to whatever you feel is appropriate to mount the text. You can edit an existing document by going to **File > Open** and then selecting your file.

Step 2: Enabling the Text Tool

1. **Find the Text Tool**: The Text tool will be at the left-hand toolbar. That is represented by an icon "**T**." You use it to type directly on your canvas. There are two kinds of text types in Photoshop that are, Point Text and Paragraph Text.

2. **Select Your Text Type:**
   - **Point** Text is perfect for a small text in a section or Title that is required to grow in a single line.
   - **Paragraph** Text is better for longer sections or paragraph formatting when the text has to be confined within a bounding box.

Step 3: Adding Point Text

1. **Choose the Point Text Tool:** With the Text Tool selected, click once on your canvas where you want to start with your text.

2. **Type Your Text:** Start typing. Immediately, your text will be written in Photoshop. To finish typing, press Enter (Return on Mac). If you need several lines, then press **Shift+Enter** for a new line within the same text box.

3. **Move and Adjust Point Text**: To move your text, select the **Move Tool** (V). Under the text layer click and drag where you want the text to sit.

Step 4: Adding Paragraph Text

1. **Create a Text Box for Paragraph Text:** Drag the mouse on the canvas to create a text box for longer passages. This will confine the text within the space defined by it, perfect for paragraphs or columns.

2. **Type and Format Your Text:** In the box, type your text. If the text happens to be more than what can fit inside the box, Photoshop automatically conceals the extra bits and pieces that one might reveal if the box is re-scaled.

3. **Resize and Reposition**: Resize by dragging the corners of the text box. Move by selecting the **Move Tool** (V) or using the arrow keys.

Step 5: Formatting Text with the Options Bar

1. **Adjust Font, Size, and Style**: The top of Photoshop has an Options bar that displays settings for fonts, font size, style - bold, italic, and alignment - left, center, right.

2. **Select a Font**: Click the font menu to see a list of your available fonts. Photoshop also supports Adobe Fonts integration if you have additional fonts available in your subscription with Creative Cloud.

3. **Adjust Font Size and Style**: You will be able to indicate the size and type of font to provide better readability or to accommodate design specifications. It shall be useful for headers and captions in case you want more prominence or emphasis.

Step 6: Advanced Text Formatting

1. **Open the Character and Paragraph Panels**: Open **Window > Character** and then **Window > Paragraph**. Through these panels, you will be able to access the more refined text attributes such as spacing, leading, kerning, and alignment options.

2. **Edit Character Settings:** In the Character panel, there are more detailed text options such as text color edits, baseline shifts, or adding underlines. This will fine-tune the look of your design.

3. **Set Paragraph Alignments**: Justification options available in the Paragraph panel for multi-line text include alignment to the left, center, and right, as well as justified. These options ensure visually appealing layouts in documents heavy with text.

Step 7: Applying Effects to Text

1. **Access Blending Options**: The text layer can be given effects such as shadow or stroke by accessing the blending options via a right-click in the Layers panel. This opens many styling options.

2. **Add a Drop Shadow:** Enable **Drop Shadow**, which will let you add depth by adjusting the angle, distance, and opacity to whatever does the trick to make it look great and more readable.

3. **Add a Stroke:** Outlining your text is possible using the Stroke option. You could adjust color, size, and position to get bold or subtle.

4. **Try out the rest of the Effects**: Other effects, like Bevel & Emboss, Gradient Overlay, and Outer Glow, give your text more personality, especially in logos and title text. Experiment with them to see what works for your design.

Step 8: Transforming and Positioning Text

1. **Free Transform to Scale and Rotate:** With the text layer selected, use the shortcut Ctrl+T (Cmd+T on Mac) to activate Free Transform. Dragging the handles of the bounding box scales rotates, or skews the text.

2. **Position Accurately:** For correct placing, choose Align Tools from the Options Bar or make manual adjustments by dragging. You can also use guides or the grid that may be turned on under **View > Show > Grid**.

Step 9: Saving and Exporting Your Text

1. **Save Your Work**: Saving the file in PSD format will keep the text layers in editable format for later editing. Go to **File > Save As**, and then choose **PSD format**.

2. **Export for Web or Print:** To export, go to **File > Export > Export As**, and choose the format needed JPEG, PNG, etc. Make use of high-resolution settings for print and standard settings for the web.

HOW TO EDIT TEXT

Follow the steps below to learn how to edit text:

Step 1: Open Your Project and Choose the Text Layer

Before editing text in Photoshop, ensure that you have your project open and the correct text layer selected. Follow these steps:

1. Open Photoshop 2025 and load your file by going to **File > Open** and selecting the project.

2. Go to the Layers Panel, and select the text layer you want to edit. Typically, each text layer has a "**T**" icon.

3. Click on the text layer to make it active. This will ensure any edits are done only to this text layer.

If you are working on a multi-layered project, it is a good idea to group similar text layers by highlighting them and hitting Ctrl+G for Windows or Cmd+G for Mac. This will allow you to keep your workspace clear of clutter.

Step 2: Select the Text Tool

Now that you have your layer selected, you'll need to activate your Text Tool to type your text.

1. On the toolbar to the left, select the **Horizontal Type Tool**, or simply press **T** on your keyboard to do so.

2. Click directly on the text you want to edit - this will insert a cursor into a text box and allow editing as one might in a typical text editor.

3. You can now type new text, delete existing text, or make other edits.

If the text you're editing is rasterized, turned into pixels rather than vector text, Photoshop will not allow you to edit it directly. You would have to recreate the text layer if it has been rasterized.

Step 3: Edit Text Content

To edit the text content:

1. With the Text Tool active and the text box highlighted, add, delete, or replace text as needed using your keyboard.

2. Click off the text box or hit Enter on Windows or Return on Mac to accept your changes.

If you ever want to keep the original text in case of a backup, highlight the layer that your text is on by right-clicking the layer and selecting **Duplicate Layer**.

Step 4: Adjusting Font and Size

Photoshop provides numerous ways to modify font characteristics. To do this:

1. After having typed text, highlight it and locate the Options Bar at the top of the screen display.

2. To select a new font, access the Font Family drop-down menu. You can either browse through the fonts in that list or start typing a font name and it will jump to that selection.

3. To adjust your font size, use the dropdown selection under Font Size in the Options Bar or simply type a specific number of your choice. Otherwise, you can resize proportionally by clicking and dragging the corner of the text box.

4. For more advanced font settings, like Horizontal Scale or Vertical Scale for taller, wider, or condensed fonts, use the Character Panel via **Window > Character**.

Step 5: Change Text Color

Changing text color:

1. With the Text Tool selected, highlight the text you want to recolor.

2. In the Options Bar, click the **Color Picker**, color swatch, and then select a new color by manually choosing, entering a hex code, or sampling color from the image by clicking on it.

3. Once you've selected the color of your liking, click **OK** to apply.

Experiment with different color gradients, shading, or overlay effects for more dynamic text styles.

Step 6: Apply Text Style and Effects

Photoshop also offers you numerous styles and effects to make your text look all the more eye-catching. You can add shadow, gradient, stroke, and more by using the Layer Styles panel, opening via:

1. Right-click the text layer in the Layers Panel and select Blending Options in the menu.
2. Here, you will be able to use various options to apply different effects.
   Examples include:
   - **Drop Shadow:** This adds a shadow behind the text, adding depth to it.
   - **Stroke**: Outlines the text. You can change its size, color, and position.
   - **Gradient Overlay**: You can add a gradient fill in the text, which can be modified according to your design.
   - **Bevel and Emboss**: This effect imparts a three-dimensional look upon the text to make it appear raised or engraved.
3. To apply each of these effects, select the checkbox beside the name, then modify the settings until satisfactory.

Note: Multiple effects combined can add to the text, but at times, too many may overwhelm the design. Keep it in balance.

Step 7: Adjust Text Spacing and Alignment

Proper spacing and proper alignment ensure that the text looks professional and is readable.

1. Open the **Character Panel** through **Window > Character**, and adjust Leading - space between lines, Tracking - space between letters, and Kerning - space between certain pairs of characters.

2. To align text, go to the **Paragraph Panel** (Window > Paragraph) and select options for **Left**, **Center**, or **Right Alignment**.

If you are dealing with big blocks of text, adjusting the spacing is a huge factor.

Step 8: Transform and Position Text

Your text can be taken to the next level by transforming and positioning it in your project.

1. Click and drag with the Move Tool to move the text layer to whatever location you would like.

2. To Rotate, hit **Ctrl+T** for **Windows** or **Cmd+T** for **Mac** operating systems. Click and drag off of the transformation box to rotate the text layer, or drag corners to size it.

3. Hit **Enter** for Windows or **Return** for Mac to apply the transformation.

If you hold down the **Shift key** while resizing, it helps to maintain the aspect ratio. Otherwise, your text would look stretched or blurry.

Step 9: Save Your Work

At the end of editing, save your work the right way:

1. Go to **File > Save As** to save your project in Photoshop's **PSD** format, preserving all layers and editability.

2. For a finished graphic, export the project as a **JPEG** or **PNG** by going to **File > Export > Export As**. Choose the appropriate format and quality based on your intended usage.

First, save a file as a PSD for continued editing and export it out for final distribution.

RESIZE THE ENTIRE TEXT ON A TYPE LAYER

Method 1: Resizing Text Using Free Transform Tool

The Free Transform Tool is the fastest way to resize a type layer. This tool lets you interactively resize text, great if you want to see real-time changes to your text's size and positioning.

1. **Open the Photoshop Document:** Open Adobe Photoshop 2025. If you haven't added text yet, create a new type layer by selecting the Type Tool - from the toolbar click anywhere in your document and type your text.

2. **Select the Type Layer**: Highlight the needed type layer from the Layers Panel to see the text preview within the layer thumbnail.

3. **Enable Free Transform**: With a type layer selected, use the keyboard shortcut Ctrl + T for Windows or Cmd + T for Mac. Then, enable the Free Transform tool. This will bound your text with a bounding box with corner and side handles.

4. Resizing Text

- To scale the text, click and drag any of the corner handles of the bounding box; holding the Shift key down will constrain the aspect ratio-meaning your text's proportions remain consistent in the process of resizing.
- If you want free-form resizing, avoid the Shift key and pull freely on the handles. Drag the bounding box inwards and outwards until the bounding box size for the text is what you would like.

5. **Commit the Transformation**: When you are satisfied with the new size, press Enter in Windows or Return in Mac to commit the transformation. This will resize your text layer.

6. **Edit if Needed:** Once you've resized the text, you can make more edits using other tools like repositioning, rotating, or applying effects.

Applying the Free Transform Tool is quick and works all right when one makes a visual adjustment but does not need the exact font size.

Method 2: Resizing Text Using the Character Panel

The Character Panel enables precise manipulation of text attributes such as font size, tracking, and leading. When you need to resize text to a specific point size, this panel is very effective.

1. **Open the Character Panel:** Click **Window > Character**. It opens the panel where one can adjust innumerable text attributes including font size.

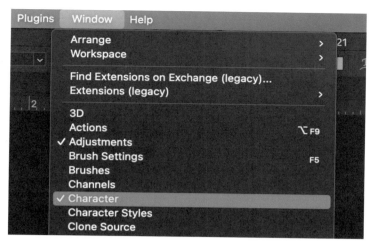

2. **Click the Text**: With the Type Tool (T) selected, click on the type layer in the Layers Panel. Click and drag over the text you want to resize or just make sure the type layer is selected if you want to resize all the text that is present on the layer.

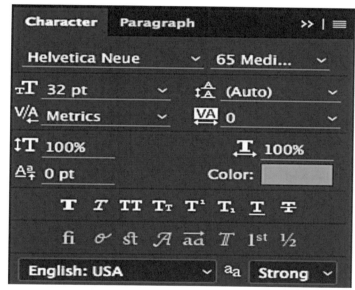

3. **Enter a New Font Size**: In the Character Panel, locate the Font Size field, you will see that it reads either "**px**" or "**pt**", by default. From here, you may enter your font size directly, or click the up and/or down arrows to increase or decrease font size incrementally.

4. **Adjust Other Properties (Optional):** You can also use the Character Panel to further adjust other properties like tracking, which is spacing between letters, and leading, which refers to line spacing. The above properties may be useful if you are resizing. You can make alterations to these values if you feel the resized text needs further adjustments.

5. **Finalize and Close the Panel:** Just click the Character Panel once you are satisfied with the size, or choose another tool. Changes will take effect immediately on your type layer.

It is worth noting that working with the Character Panel comes in particularly handy when having to resize numerous type layers to match, or regularly maintaining text formatting for specific design projects.

Method 3: Resizing Text via the Properties Panel

Another straightforward option for adjusting text size is available through the Properties Panel within Adobe Photoshop 2025. This will present a more intuitive, visually oriented means of resurfacing.

1. **Open the Properties Panel:** Open the Properties Panel from **Window > Properties** if it isn't already open.

2. **Choose the Type Layer:** In the Layers Panel, click to highlight the type layer that you want to resize. The Properties Panel will display type layer-specific options, such as font settings and the size of text.

3. **Adjust the Text Size**: In the Properties Panel, locate the Font Size slider or input box. You can directly type in a size or use the slider to increase or decrease the size of your text until you achieve the intended look.

4. **Improve the Text (Optional):** You will realize that, in the Properties Panel, you can modify font type, color, and alignment for texts. Thus, this makes the panel useful in text modification. More modifications can be done here.

5. **Confirm the Changes**: Once done with the necessary changes, your type layer will instantly update itself with the changed settings. Simply click outside the Properties Panel to advance further with the editing of other design elements.

The Properties Panel proves helpful in instances when you have opened several design elements and wish to resize text as quickly as possible without necessarily toggling between tools very often.

USING EMOJI FONTS

Step 1: Setting Up a New Document

- Open the document in Photoshop through **File > New**, or for quick access, Ctrl+N for Windows/Cmd+N for Mac. Now you have to choose between your preferred width, height, and resolution because it depends for what reason you design this.
- Set the resolution high, something like 300 pixels per inch, because this project involves emojis, and with such resolution, it would be nice and sharp. Once you have set up your document, click **Create**.

Step 2: Accessing the Type Tool

- Select the **Type Tool**, from the left-hand toolbar (it looks like a "T") or hit T on your keyboard. Click anywhere in your document where you'd like text to be.
- A text box opens that can later be adjusted as you would like to reposition or resize your text.

Step 3: Choosing an Emoji Font

- With the Type Tool selected, click the Options Bar at the top of the screen. Here, you can select your font. Adobe has several fonts that support emojis to choose from, such as Apple Color Emoji (Mac only), Segoe UI Emoji (Windows), and other Adobe fonts that are compatible with emoji characters.
- Choose an emoji (supporting font to get started). If you're unsure which to use, go ahead with Segoe UI Emoji (or its equivalent on Mac) since this is one of the most common fonts.

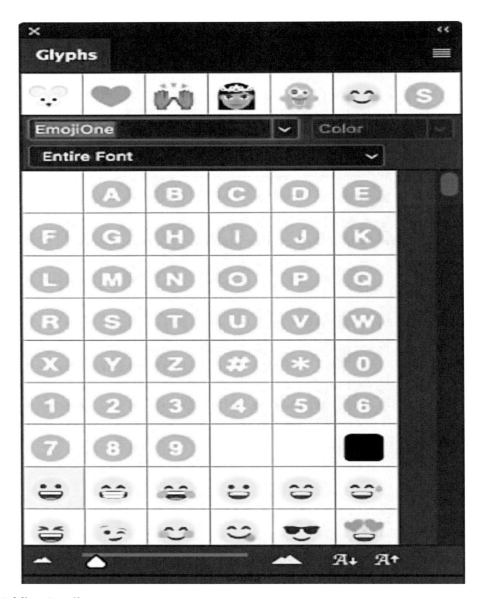

Step 4: Adding Emojis

- With your emoji font set, let's start adding the emojis to your design. Right-click inside your text box and select **Emoji & Symbols** (for Mac or Windows) + Period (.) for Windows. Immediately, a pop-up window will appear with the emoji picker already opened on one of the many categories, such as smileys, animals, food, and many others. Just click on the emoji you want to insert, and voilà; it will appear in your text box.

- Or, you can easily copy the emojis from any online source or a text editor that supports emojis and simply paste them into Photoshop.

Step 5: Styling Your Emoji Text

- Once you have placed the emojis, you can format them as you would regular text using Photoshop. Open the Character Panel via **Window > Character**. Change the size, tracking, and leading by adjusting the respective icons.
- **Note: Emoji Limitations**
  Not all emoji fonts support traditional styling options such as changing color. Emoji fonts are typically color bitmap fonts and as such appear in one set form. You can, however, scale, rotate, adjust opacity, or apply effects in Photoshop.

Step 6: Placing and Scaling the Emoji Text

- To move the emoji textbox, hit V on your keyboard to select the Move Tool. Click and drag your text box to position it on the canvas.
- To resize, use Ctrl+T for Windows or Cmd+T for Mac to activate Free Transform mode. This will give you an actively scaling text box by tugging at the corners. Holding down the Shift key maintains the proportions.

Step 7: Adding Extra Effects

- Additional effects can be added to the emojis. Highlight your emoji text layer and go to **Layer > Layer Style > Blending Options.**
- You can add Drop Shadows, Strokes, Outer Glow, or even Bevel & Emboss to give the emojis some depth.

Step 8: Rasterizing the Emoji Layer (Optional)

- For more complex transformations and advanced blend mode use on the emojis, you would more than likely need to rasterize the text layer. To do so, right-click the emoji text layer in the Layers Panel and select **Rasterize Type**.
- Note that by doing this, you will be converting the text into pixels. The text will no longer be editable as a font but will be fully editable as an image layer.

Step 9: Save and Export Your Design

- Save your design once you are satisfied with your emoji design. Go to File > Save As and choose PSD format if you want to keep all the layers that are presently visible in the design for Photoshop to edit later.
- For web or print sharing, **go to File > Export > Export As and select the format you need - JPEG, PNG, or TIFF.**

CHAPTER TEN

EXPORT, SAVE, AND FILE MANAGEMENT OPTIONS

SAVE YOUR FILES IN PHOTOSHOP

Step 1: Complete Your Editing

Save first after you have completed editing your file in Photoshop. Make sure to go through layers, color adjustments, or other effects you may have used. This will ensure that if you save your file in Photoshop (.PSD) format, all the layers, masks, and other editable elements will be saved so that you can always revisit and refine any work.

Step 2: Open the Save Options

1. **Locate the File Menu:** This typically is along the top left-hand side of your screen and provides options related to files.

2. **Select Save or Save As**: If you haven't saved the file previously, Save As is recommended since you will be able to choose a new format or location. You can click on Save if you've already saved the file and only want to overwrite the current version with your newer changes.

If this is the first time you save the file, it's highly recommended to click on **Save As** to determine the format and location thoughtfully.

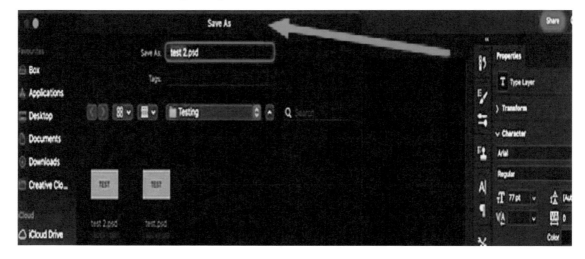

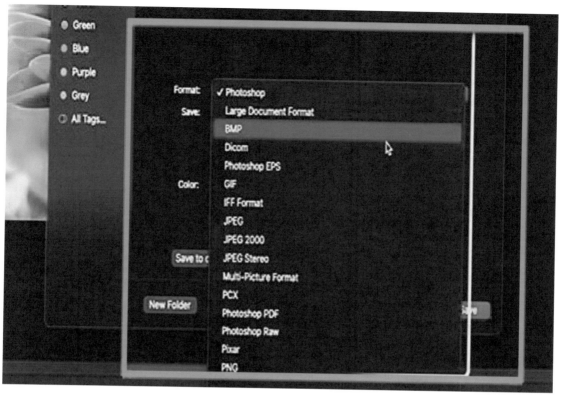

Step 3: Choose the Save Location

This opens a dialog box where you need to choose a folder in which you need to save the file. You can directly save it to your computer or even on cloud storage, like Adobe Creative Cloud, so that it would be easier for any device to access.

1. **Computer Save**: Point out the folder on your hard drive. Make it an organized location so it is easier for you to find your work later.

2. **Save to the Cloud**: If you have an Adobe Creative Cloud account you can save work directly to the cloud. The cloud is where you want to save your work if you will be accessing or sharing from multiple devices or locations.

Step 4: Select the File Format Option

Within Photoshop you have several file format options that each serve different purposes.

Here is an overview:

1. **Photoshop (.PSD):** The default format is with all the layers and everything is still editable in its original form. You should choose PSD if you would like to reopen the file at some point in the future for editing.

2. **JPEG (.JPG):** Best to finalize the image and compress it. JPEGs are much smaller and, therefore, quite easy to share with other devices or software; thus, you should choose JPEG if you intend to share the file on a website or social media.

3. **PNG (.PNG):** PNG supports a variety of colors and transparency, which makes that file type perfect for graphics and logos. For web graphics, if the background needs to be transparent, then create those in PNG.

4. **TIFF (.TIF):** The TIFF files are very good in quality and detail. Choose TIFF when you want to create print work or high-quality image archives.

5. **PDF (.PDF):** Use PDFs when you need to create a viewable document that maintains all the elements created in Photoshop. This is great to share in print-friendly format or as an attachment via email.

After choosing the format you want, click on the **Options** icon, to adjust the quality in case of a JPEG format or the amount of compression applied in case of a TIFF format.

Step 5: Setup Additional Options

Each format in Photoshop has its options:

- **JPEG Quality:** From 1 (Low) to 12 (Maximum), the better the quality, the more detailed it would be, while the bigger the file.

- **PNG Compression:** PNG files are lossless, meaning whatever information is not lost because of the huge compression; you can, however, make some optimization for a size smaller.

- **TIFF Compression:** Compresses using LZW and ZIP without sacrificing much of their quality.

- **PDF Options:** You can include layers, vectors, and high-quality options along with password-protecting it in PDF.

Step 6: Save the File

1. After setting your settings, you can save the file in your desired format by clicking **Save or OK.**

2. If there is a warning or prompt, choose options carefully so all the elements you are using, layers, color profiles, etc., will be preserved.

3. Be patient when saving as it may take several seconds if you have a high-resolution project.

Step 7: Backing Up Your Files

- Once one has saved, it is a good practice to backup. One might use Adobe's Save a Copy option to create a copy of the file in a different format that is ideal for sharing a flattened version of the file while maintaining an editable file. One might also copy the file onto an external drive or to Adobe Cloud backup.

EXPORT FILES IN PHOTOSHOP

Step 1: Open the Export Menu

- When you are done with your project in Adobe Photoshop, under the File menu at the top left of your screen you have several options under Export.
- You can click on **Export As** or **Quick Export As [File Type]** depending on whether you want a quick export or one that allows you to customize more options.

Step 2: Select the Export As Option

- Clicking on Export As will open a new window in Photoshop with a preview of your image; several settings will appear. This option gives more precision in managing your file, where the user can work with format, size, resolution, and color options.
- You will see a preview of your image on the left and several adjustable parameters on the right. The new feature works when the user wants more control over the export.

Step 3: Choose the File Format

The first option in the Export As window is the format of the file. There are several formats available within Photoshop, each serving a different purpose:

- **JPEG**: This is good for photos on the web and social media; it allows adjustment for quality to reduce file size.

- **PNG**: Great for images that require transparency, such as logos or graphics cut out from their backgrounds.

- **GIF**: Used for simple animations or low-resolution graphics.

- **SVG**: Best for scalable vector graphics applied in web design.

- **PDF**: This is for printing at its best, if layers and the highest quality graphics are used.

Choose Whatever is closest to your implementation. If you make an image for the web, JPEG or PNG would be best. Consider SVG or GIF if your design involves vectors and animations.

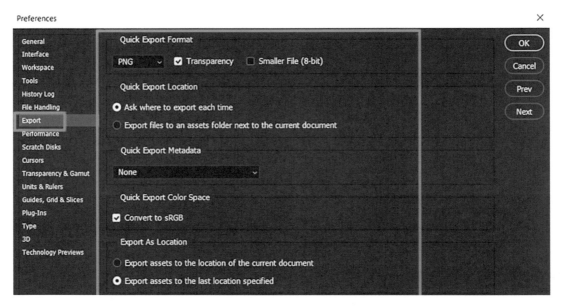

Step 4: Set the Image Size and Scale

- The next one is Image Size. You can change the Width and Height by placing appropriate values in pixels. Right underneath these fields, there is a Scale option that lets you export the image in different percentages: 50%, 100%, 200%, etc. Scaling options are very useful for responsive web design, where you'll need to have multiple resolutions.
- For example, if printing high-resolution images, select 100% Scale and enter the necessary pixel dimensions. Scaling down usually results in smaller file sizes; however, that can reduce the quality of the image.

Step 5: Adjust the Resolution

- The resolution is in pixels per inch, which controls the clarity.
- For web use, **the standard is 72 PPI**, creating smaller files optimized for fast loading across different devices.
- **For print**, the recommended is **300 PPI** to make sure the image will show clarity and details in your final printed material. Change the resolution according to your target output.

Step 6: Save the File with Quality Settings

- In the case of file formats like JPEG, Photoshop has a Quality slider where you can balance the trade-off between file size and the clarity of your images.
- The higher the quality, the sharper your image will be but the larger its size; the lower the quality, the less space it takes but the poorer the quality of the shot. It is very handy when you are preparing an image for websites or social media, as the smaller the file size is, the sooner it will appear on a screen.

Step 7: Set Export Preferences for Transparency

- Formats like PNG support the transparency options. If your project requires you to have transparent backgrounds, then this option should be checked to retain transparency.
- **Note** that JPEG does not support transparency, so this option will not appear if you are exporting as a JPEG.

Step 8: Choose Export Destination and File Name

- Once you have your settings personalized, click **Export All** at the bottom right to select a destination folder. A dialog box will pop up asking you to choose in which location on your computer you want to save the exported file.
- Give a file name and make sure the extension is, for example, .jpg or.png depending on which one you chose.

Step 9: Check the Export Preview

- Photoshop provides a real-time Preview of how the image will look with the chosen settings. Make it a habit to stop and take one last look at this preview before exporting and making those last-minute adjustments.
- This is convenient just to view the visual appearance of the image with the selected resolution and quality.

Step 10: Export and Save

- Click on **Export All** to finish the export. Now, Photoshop will save your image with the settings you have specified, and the export will be complete.
- Now, check the exported file in an external viewer or application.

HOW TO TRANSFER DESIGNS FROM PHOTOSHOP TO ILLUSTRATOR

Understand the Difference Between Photoshop and Illustrator

Well, before proceeding with technical steps, it is rather important to know the main difference between the two pieces of software: the fact that Photoshop mainly represents a raster-based application, which is perfect for photo editing and pixel-based graphics, while Illustrator is vector-based, allowing infinite scalability of graphics. Such knowledge will help you choose the right format and settings when transferring the designs.

Preparing Your Photoshop File for Transfer

Organize your layers and assets in Photoshop to make the transfer to Illustrator as smooth as possible.

1. **Clean Up Your Layers:** Do this by cleaning up your layers: naming them appropriately, grouping similar layers, and deleting any unnecessary elements.

2. **Adjust Resolution and Color Mode**: Adjust the resolution and color mode to the desired resolution for Photoshop and select the right color mode, either CMYK for printing or RGB for web use.

3. **Use Smart Objects for Scalability**: Using Smart Objects on elements that may need to be resized will keep its quality when resizing it in Illustrator.

Step 3: Export from Photoshop to Illustrator

You have several options as to how you're transferring elements from Photoshop to Illustrator. Here are the best ways to do this:

Method 1: Copy and Paste

1. In Photoshop, select an element or group of elements you want to transfer.

2. Copy the selected elements using **Ctrl+C for Windows** or **Cmd+C for Mac.**

3. Go back to Illustrator and paste using Ctrl+V for Windows or Cmd+V for Mac.

4. Illustrator will pop up a dialog box to paste as a "**Compound Shape," "Compound Path,"** or "**Flat Image.**" To retain the layer structures, choose "**Compound Shape.**" The positive side of this approach is that it works great for elements based on vectors, though it does have a negative side of rasterizing some of the effects.

Method 2: Use Export As

1. In Photoshop, head to File > Export > Export As….

2. Choose from the following file types as desired:
   - PNG for web-based or transparent background graphics.
   - SVG for scalable, vector-based artwork.
   - PDF format for a document type that includes vector information.

3. Click on the Export option after selecting your preferred format and save the file.

4. Finally, open Illustrator and select **File > Open** to import the exported file.

Method 3: Export as PSD File

How to maintain the layer structure of Photoshop in Illustrator:

1. Save your project in Photoshop in **.PSD format.**

2. Then, open Illustrator; go to the menu, **File > Open,** and select your **.PSD file.**

3. A dialogue box opens in Illustrator, asking if you'd like to convert the layers into objects or flatten them. Choose **Convert Layers to Objects to** retain the layers.

4. Click OK to import the file with layers, so that you can edit each of your elements in Illustrator individually.

Step 4: Editing Imported Elements within Illustrator

Since you already imported these elements, you can easily go into Illustrator and edit the design elements:

1. **Modify Colors and Textures**: Since Illustrator is vector-based, colors and effects may appear different. In this case, you'd want to modify them via the Color Panel or Swatches.

2. **Cleaning up the Paths**: If your paths aren't exactly as you need them to be, you may want to fine-tune them further using the Pen or Direct Selection Tool.

3. **Scaling Objects**: Although you may have imported rasterized elements, the quality won't improve if they are scaled in Illustrator. Make sure you work with vector shapes if you need scalable graphics.

Step 5: Bringing the Design Back into Photoshop

If at this point you want to bring your Illustrator design back into Photoshop after making edits, here's how you can do it:

1. Select all or some of the layers to be exported in Illustrator.

2. Navigate to **File > Export > Export As**... and set the file format as PSD, which will retain all your layers.

3. Once the export is complete, open Photoshop and load the edited file through File > Open.

4. This way, Photoshop will import your design with layers intact for further editing.

You also can copy directly from Illustrator and paste it into Photoshop as a Smart Object; this way, you can resize and edit the design without affecting its quality.

Step 6: Refine Your Design in Photoshop

After importing, fix everything that needs to be done to your satisfaction:

- **Edit Colors or Add Filters:** Filters and color adjustments within Photoshop put special touches on to make your design perfect.
- **Apply Effects:** Apply layer styles to complete the look, such as drop shadow, gradient, or blending options.

CHAPTER ELEVEN

TROUBLESHOOTING, PERFORMANCE, OPTIMIZATION, AND BEST PRACTICES

Common Photoshop Issues and How to Resolve Them

Photoshop is one of the most powerful and popular applications related to image editing and graphic design. Like all software programs, there are also common problems with this software. Here are a few.

1. Photoshop Running Slowly or Lagging

As the performance of Photoshop is poor, this can damage the productivity of a person using it when working on big projects. This can also relate to a memory problem or the performance of the working system.

- **Step 1: Increase RAM Allocation**
  Go to **Edit > Preferences > Performance** and increase the amount of RAM allocated for Photoshop. It may be set too low by default if you have ample RAM on your computer.
- **Step 2: Scratch Disk Optimization**
  Set a fast, high-capacity drive as the scratch disk under Preferences > Scratch Disks. Avoid using system drives because they slow everything down.
- **Step 3: Limit History States and Cache Levels**
  Too much history or too high a cache eats up the memory. In Preferences, Performance adjusts these to reasonable limits.
- **Step 4: Disable Unnecessary Plugins**
  Extra plugins slow down performance. Under **Edit**, go to **Plugins** and disable or remove any extra plugins not in use.

2. Photoshop Crashing or Not Responding

Of course, a crashing problem gets highly frustrating, especially if you have to work on urgent projects. Now, let's see how to troubleshoot.

- **Step 1: Update Photoshop and Your System**
  Make sure that Photoshop is updated, as well as your Operating System. Usually, Adobe releases patches for bug fixes and compatibility issues.
- **Step 2: Reset Preferences**
  Corrupted preferences will crash the program. The application will restart its preferences after hitting **Ctrl + Alt + Shift** for Windows, or **Command + Option + Shift** for Mac when opening Photoshop.

- **Step 3: Check Incompatible Hardware**

  An outdated or incompatible graphic card may be the problem. Update the drivers or adjust the Photoshop settings under **Edit > Preferences > Performance** by unchecking Use Graphics Processor to check if the issue gets resolved.

- **Step 4: Clear Scratch Disk**

  Full scratch disks can cause crashes. Free up the space by deleting unwanted files in the drive being used for the scratch disk or pointing to a new drive in the **Preferences > Scratch Disks**.

3. **Tools Not Working Correctly**

At times, the tools in Photoshop don't work right. This could simply be because the settings have been corrupted, or some other minor glitch is going on.

- **Step 1: Reset Tool**

  Right-click the icon of the tool in the toolbar and click on Reset Tool; it will reset to default.

- **Step 2: Layer Not Locked**

  Sometimes tools may not work properly because a layer that you are trying to edit is locked. To unlock, simply click the padlock icon beside the layer in the Layers panel.

- **Step 3: Disable Extra Tools**

  If you have multiple devices enabled, including that of the stylus and other extensions, it might interfere with the way tools behave in Photoshop. Try disabling other devices and restart Photoshop to see if it goes away.

4. **Problems Exporting Files**

Problems exporting files include but are not limited to failure to export mainly when the file size is huge or the format is uncommon. The troubleshooting includes the following:

- **Step 1: Instead of Export, 'Save As'**

  If the normal function of Export As is not going well, then you can go ahead and save the file with the desired format by opening it in **File > Save As**.

- **Step 2: Flatten Layers**

  Large files with many layers may refuse to export well. Once you flatten your image by going to **Layer > Flatten Image**, try again with exporting.

- **Step 3: Reduce File Size**

  This will decrease the file size either by shrinking the dimensions of your image or by reducing the quality settings in the export dialogue. Large files are beyond Photoshop's limitations.

5. **Photoshop Freezes When Launching**

When launching, if Photoshop freezes, the problem may be one of three: conflicted plugins, corrupted fonts, and preference issues.

- **Step 1: Disable Plugins**

  Launch Photoshop without plugins by holding Shift during the opening of the application. This will show you if there is some sort of plugin that causes it.
- **Step 2: Clear Font Cache**

  Corrupt fonts are an issue sometimes. Clear the font cache from your font folder by erasing any corrupt files or cache folders.
- **Step 3: Reset Preferences**

  Resetting the preferences is done by holding **Ctrl + Alt + Shift** for Windows and Command + Option + Shift for Mac upon launch. This sorts out problems upon launch often.

SOME TIPS FOR SPEEDING UP PHOTOSHOP PERFORMANCE

Step 1: Optimize Photoshop's Performance Preferences

Photoshop has allowed you to decide how the application should utilize system resources to improve performance. To access the Performance Preferences in Photoshop, navigate to **Edit > Preferences > Performance**:

- **Adjust Memory Usage:** Photoshop uses RAM aggressively. It is recommended that you assign about 70-85% of your available RAM to Photoshop, depending on how much RAM your system has. Never use all the available RAM, as this could make your system unstable.
- **Graphics Processor Settings**: If the graphics processor is enabled, it can accelerate many tools and operations. This helps immensely when working on designs in 3D or high-resolution images. Open the **Performance section** and ensure that the option Use Graphics Processor is checked. Further advanced settings can be done here according to your computer's GPU for performance enhancements.
- **History and Cache settings**: Increase the cache levels if you work with huge documents, such as 4-8 levels for large documents, or decrease on smaller files to speed up the loading time of opening them. Choose a **Cache Pre-set** good enough for your purposes in your workflow such as Web/UI Design, Default, or Huge Pixel Dimensions.

Step 2: Manage Scratch Disks

Scratch Disks: Scratch disks are used by default in Photoshop when the application reaches its maximum RAM capacity. To configure your scratch disk in Photoshop, use a fast secondary drive; if possible, an SSD will be ideal in performance. To do this, follow the steps below:

Open **Edit > Preferences > Scratch Disks**. Set your scratch disk to be one of the fastest drives that have more available space. If possible, avoid installing Photoshop on the same disk to improve performance.

Step 3: Use Efficient Document and File Settings

The following are the file settings that help improve Photoshop's performance by a great degree:

- **Lower Document Resolution**: Try to refrain from using more than what is necessary when it comes to resolution for web projects. Typically, 72 PPI gets the job done for the web. Save your high-resolution files only when you need them for print.

- **Minimize Layers and Smart Objects:** The heavier the file with numerous layers, the painfully slow it makes Photoshop. Merging layers where possible and a limited number of Smart Objects unless needed is good practice.

- **Save Large Files as PSB**: If your file is greater than 2 GB, you may want to save it as a PSB instead of saving it as a PSD. The PSBs handle larger and bigger files without lagging.

Step 4: Close Unused Documents and Purge Memory

Opening several documents in Photoshop makes the software's performance slow. To avoid this,

- **Close Unused Documents:** This will release the memory resources that will be utilized in the currently working project.

- **Purge**: In the Edit menu, there is also Purge, which clears the clipboard history or other caches that may be occupying your RAM. This will liberate some of your memory, but keep in mind it's irreversible, so save your work in advance.

Step 5: Adjust Interface and Switch Off Unnecessary Features

Photoshop has a lot of features that the average user will never use:

- **Disable Animated Zoom**: Go to preferences, and tools, and click on animated Zoom. This often smooths navigation because every unnecessary use of animations is turned off.

- **Turn Off Preview Options:** If you are working with high-resolution images, on layers, turn off thumbnail previews. These little previews suck up processing power from your computer.

- **Simplify the Workspace:** Close panels you don't use regularly. A clean interface helps lower the processing needs of your computer and lets Photoshop put more resources into tasks currently in use.

Step 6: Update Your Hardware and Keep Software Updated

Before trying the ways mentioned above to make full use of Photoshop, you first of all need to ensure that your software and hardware are up-to-date. This you can do in the following way:

- **Update Photoshop Periodically:** Adobe periodically releases certain performance updates. Make sure that Photoshop stays updated. Go to **Help > Updates** to check for any available updates.

- **Hardware Upgrade**: Just add more RAM, add higher capacity to an SSD, or even use a dedicated graphics card if you work with complex files regularly. For Photoshop 2025, Adobe's minimum requirements stand at 16 GB RAM for ultimate performance, though 32 GB or more is recommended for heavy tasks.

Step 7: Optimizing System Settings for Photoshop

Improve the performance of Photoshop by optimizing your system further:

- Close background applications are not necessary for your workflow.

- Change your computer's power settings to High-Performance mode. For the Windows computer, this would be a **Control Panel > Power Options**. On Mac, it's located in the "**Energy Saver**" setting.

CONCLUSION

Adobe Photoshop 2025 is truly a powerhouse born out of innovation in digital artistry and design, pushing the boundaries with advanced tools that answer creative needs both for professionals and enthusiasts alike. With AI-driven enhancements, Photoshop 2025 makes workflows transformative wherein tasks that would have taken so much time and effort are now done with greater swiftness and intuitiveness. From the automated selection and content-aware fills to the newly improved neural filters, this latest release lets the user make perfect edits with unprecedented ease and allows their creativity to run riot.

Cloud-based collaboration has further redefined the way one knows Photoshop. This enables teams to make contributions in real-time, regardless of where the creative lives. Designers, photographers, and digital artists easily share projects, view feedback, and edit simultaneously for maximum efficiency and in-group creativity. More than this, though, the enhanced 3D and augmented reality capabilities of Photoshop 2025 open new dimensions for digital creators by equipping them with just the right tool to create immersive experiences in the name of a highly virtual world.

Adobe Photoshop 2025 represents not only the change that is happening but continues to shape the future of digital art. It's a powerhouse that lets creatives push the boundaries with design, yet it's true to the level of quality and precision that people have learned to expect from Adobe. Looking ahead, the tools and capabilities in this version provide an exciting foundation for digital creatives to come, sparking new ideas and possibilities across industries. Accessible, innovative, and collaborative, Photoshop 2025 is not just software; it's a gateway to boundless creativity.

INDEX

Made in the USA
Columbia, SC
03 June 2025

58866486R00102